100 AMAZING FACTS ABOUT INDIA

2024, Marc Dresgui

Index

Introduction 6
Fact 1 - Kashmir saffron, the most precious of spices 7
Fact 2 - Kutch's white Rann desert stretches as far as the eye can see 8
Fact 3 - The national peacock dances in the rain 9
Fact 4 - The Rewa white tiger is extremely rare 10
Fact 5 - The Deccan Plateau, one of the world's oldest formations 11
Fact 6 - The Spiti valley resembles a lunar landscape 12
Fact 7 - The Western Ghats, one of the world's oldest chains 13
Fact 8 - The concept of mathematical infinity has roots in India 14
Fact 9 - Golconde Fort, renowned for its acoustics 15
Fact 10 - The Taj Mahal changes color with the light 17
Fact 11 - The Chambal River is home to rare crocodiles 18
Fact 12 - Diwali lights up the whole of India every year 19
Fact 13 - The Brahmaputra passes through three countries 20
Fact 14 - India's parliament sits in a circular building 21
Fact 15 - Ghee, the clarified butter essential to Indian cuisine 22
Fact 16 - The Kumbh Mela brings together 100 million people 23
Fact 17 - Monkeys protect temples in India 24
Fact 18 - Delhi's Red Fort, witness to the Mughal emperors 25
Fact 19 - The bhut jolokia pepper is one of the strongest 26
Fact 20 - The Sarasvati, India's mythical vanishing river 28
Fact 21 - Patanjali codified yoga millennia ago 29
Fact 22 - The Sundarbans are home to unique swimming tigers 30
Fact 23 - Mehrangarh fort has remained impregnable for centuries 31
Fact 24 - The Indian elephant is sacred in Hinduism 32
Fact 25 - Holi, the world-famous festival of colors 33
Fact 26 - The dosa is a popular giant pancake 34
Fact 27 - Thar welcomes camels adapted to arid conditions 35
Fact 28 - The Indian emblem inspired by Ashoka's lions 36
Fact 29 - Thali offers an explosion of Indian flavors 37
Fact 30 - Kaziranga National Park and its one-horned rhinos 39
Fact 31 - India has 22 recognized official languages 40
Fact 32 - The Nilgiri is home to famous tea plantations 41
Fact 33 - India is home to the world's largest democracy 42
Fact 34 - The Himalayas influence India's climate 43
Fact 35 - India launched a mission to Mars in 2013 44
Fact 36 - The compass used for the first time in India 45
Fact 37 - The Brihadeswara temple is made entirely of granite 46
Fact 38 - The Lotus Temple looks like a huge flower 47
Fact 39 - The decimal system was invented in India 48
Fact 40 - Sundarbans mangroves naturally filter water 50
Fact 41 - Chess was invented in India 51
Fact 42 - Extreme temperatures in the Thar Desert 52
Fact 43 - Mount Abu, an oasis in the middle of the desert 53

Fact 44 - The king cobra detects movement with its tongue..........54
Fact 45 - India produces the largest quantity of curry in the world............55
Fact 46 - The Siachen glacier is the highest in the world................56
Fact 47 - India has the world's largest population of sacred cows 57
Fact 48 - The Kailasa temple is carved entirely out of rock..........58
Fact 49 - Chapatis are Indian yeast-free wafers 59
Fact 50 - The Akshardham temple is the largest in the world 61
Fact 51 - Cotton grown for the first time in India 62
Fact 52 - The Golden Temple of Amritsar is covered in real gold 63
Fact 53 - The red panda protected in the state of Sikkim 64
Fact 54 - India is home to the world's largest wild elephant sanctuary 65
Fact 55 - Raksha Bandhan, a festival celebrating fraternal ties................66
Fact 56 - The Western Ghats are teeming with biodiversity 67
Fact 57 - The Victoria Memorial, a vestige of colonial India 68
Fact 58 - India is the world's largest mango producer................................69
Fact 59 - India's Constitution is one of the longest in the world 70
Fact 60 - The Qûtb Minâr tower, India's tallest minaret................................72
Fact 61 - More than 1,600 languages spoken in India................................73
Fact 62 - Basmati rice has a uniquely distinctive fragrance..............74
Fact 63 - The Silk Roads passed through India 75
Fact 64 - The forests of the Western Ghats are teeming with biodiversity....76
Fact 65 - India invented the samosa, a tasty snack 77
Fact 66 - Dholes are incredibly intelligent hunters 78
Fact 67 - The Sundarbans are home to hundreds of animal species............79
Fact 68 - The Deccan Plateau, one of the world's oldest formations...........80
Fact 69 - Hyderabad's iconic Charminar 81
Fact 70 - Andaman tribes are among the most isolated in the world..........83
Fact 71 - Ganesh Chaturthi, celebrated with giant statues........................84
Fact 72 - Navratri celebrates the victory of good over evil 85
Fact 73 - Jaisalmer Fort, a citadel in the desert 86
Fact 74 - Yoga has its roots in sacred texts 87
Fact 75 - Sanskrit, one of the world's oldest languages 88
Fact 76 - Asia's largest tulip garden in Kashmir 89
Fact 77 - The Himalayas influence India's climate...90
Fact 78 - The Ganges is home to the freshwater dolphin 91
Fact 79 - Himalayan rivers spring from millennia-old glaciers.....................92
Fact 80 - Ladakh, famous for its icy desert landscapes 94
Fact 81 - The Yamuna is considered a sacred goddess 95
Fact 82 - Sushruta, pioneer of plastic surgery in India 96
Fact 83 - The Silk Roads ran through India..97
Fact 84 - Meghalaya's underground river remains a mystery 98
Fact 85 - The zero discovered by Indian mathematician Aryabhata.............99
Fact 86 - Monkeys protect temples in India..100
Fact 87 - The Chambal River is home to rare crocodiles..............................101
Fact 88 - India has the world's largest postal network 102
Fact 89 - Kangchenjunga, the world's third highest mountain 103
Fact 90 - Lake Loktak is the world's only floating lake................................105

Fact 91 - The king cobra detects movement with its tongue 106
Fact 92 - The Sarasvati, India's mythical vanishing river 107
Fact 93 - Konark's Sun temple, dedicated to the sun god 108
Fact 94 - Andaman tribes are among the most isolated in the world 109
Fact 95 - Mehrangarh fort has remained impregnable for centuries 110
Fact 96 - India has the longest national highway, NH44 111
Fact 97 - The Kumbh Mela gathers 100 million people 112
Fact 98 - Holi, the world-famous festival of colors 113
Fact 99 - The Thar Desert is home to desert foxes 114
Fact 100 - The cheetah reintroduced in India after 70 years 116
Conclusion 117
Quiz 118
Answers 121

"India has two million gods and worships every single one of them."

- Mark Twain

Introduction

Welcome to a journey through one of the world's most fascinating countries: India. In this book, you'll discover 100 Amazing Facts that reveal the richness of its culture, history and natural wonders. India, with its infinite diversity, never ceases to amaze. Whether you're curious about its thousand-year-old past or its modern innovations, these pages will open the doors to a world both ancient and vibrant.

India is a land of contrasts, where tradition meets modernity. From the majestic palaces of the Mughal emperors to centuries-old temples dedicated to countless divinities, every corner of this vast territory abounds with treasures to explore. But there's more to India than its grandiose monuments. It is also the cradle of mathematical, scientific and philosophical concepts that have shaped the world.

This book will guide you through breathtaking landscapes, from the Himalayan peaks to the icy deserts of Ladakh and the lush forests of the Sundarbans. He'll also introduce you to unique wildlife, such as the one-horned rhinoceros and the snow leopard. But India is also a land of bustling cities, colorful festivals and spicy flavors that awaken the senses.

These 100 Facts will help you understand how India has combined its deep roots with contemporary dynamism. This journey through the ages will reveal unexpected aspects of this complex and fascinating country. Whether you already know India or are discovering it for the first time, these anecdotes will pique your curiosity and enrich your vision of this Asian giant.

Prepare to be amazed and inspired. India can't be summed up in a few words, but through these 100 Facts, you'll plunge into an adventure where every detail reveals a little more of the magic and depth of this unique country. Come on board with us, and let yourself be carried away by the incredible India.

Marc Dresqui

Fact 1 - Kashmir saffron, the most precious of spices

Saffron is often called red gold. This nickname is due not only to its color, but also to its exceptional value. Kashmir saffron, grown in northern India, is recognized as one of the world's finest. This spice is extracted from crocus flowers, and it's the red stigmas, three per flower, that are harvested by hand. This painstaking process explains why saffron is so rare and expensive. It takes around 150,000 flowers to produce just one kilogram of saffron.

Renowned for its intense color, saffron is also appreciated for its unique flavor and distinctive aroma. In the kitchen, it is used to flavor dishes such as biryani, a spicy rice that is very popular in India. In addition to cooking, it is also used in religious ceremonies and traditional Indian rituals, further enhancing its cultural significance. Its ability to color dishes a bright yellow while adding a subtle touch makes it a prized spice.

Saffron cultivation in Kashmir dates back many centuries, and is strongly linked to the region's history. According to historical accounts, Persian traders introduced saffron cultivation to the Kashmir valley over 2,000 years ago. Since then, the families of this region have passed on their know-how from generation to generation. The valley's unique climate, with its cold winters and mild summers, allows crocus flowers to flourish in ideal conditions.

In addition to its culinary qualities, saffron is also used in traditional Indian medicine, Ayurveda. It is renowned for its therapeutic benefits. Some believe that saffron helps improve digestion, acts as a natural anti-inflammatory and can even have a calming effect on the mind. Many contemporary studies seek to scientifically confirm saffron's health benefits.

Kashmir saffron is much more than just a spice. It represents a local treasure that reflects India's rich biodiversity. The saffron fields in bloom, which tint the valley purple every autumn, are a unique sight, attracting the attention of visitors from all over the world.

Fact 2 - Kutch's white Rann desert stretches as far as the eye can see

The Rann of Kutch, located in the state of Gujarat, is one of the most unique deserts in India and the world. This salt desert stretches as far as the eye can see over thousands of square kilometers, creating a surreal landscape that changes with the seasons. During the monsoon season, the region is flooded, forming an immense salt plain, while in winter, the ground dries out to reveal an almost unreal expanse of brilliant white, similar to a sea of crystals.

The word "Rann" means "desert" in Hindi, and Kutch is a semi-arid region bordered by the Arabian Sea to the west. This white desert has fascinated travelers and explorers for centuries. During the day, sunlight reflects off the salt crystals, creating brilliant reflections that transform the landscape into an immense mirror. At nightfall, when the full moon shines, the desert seems to light up naturally, a spectacle that attracts visitors from all over the world.

The Rann of Kutch is not only an extraordinary place for its landscapes, but also for its unique biodiversity. Despite its arid and barren appearance, this region is home to fascinating animal species, such as the Indian wild ass, a protected species that lives in the vast expanses of this desert. Numerous migratory birds, including flamingos, come every year to take advantage of this temporarily humid habitat during the monsoon season.

The Rann of Kutch is also rich in history. For centuries, this region has been inhabited by local communities who have learned to adapt to this extreme climate. The artisans of Kutch are particularly famous for their textile work, especially their colorful embroidery and weaving techniques, which contrast with the dazzling whiteness of the desert. These craft traditions live on today, and the inhabitants continue to live in harmony with this spectacular landscape.

Every year, the government of Gujarat organizes the "Rann Utsav", a festival celebrating the culture and natural beauty of this region. For several weeks, the desert becomes a meeting place where music, dance and local crafts are showcased, attracting visitors who come to discover this natural wonder in a festive atmosphere. The Rann of Kutch is much more than a salt desert, it's a place where nature and culture meet in dazzling harmony.

Fact 3 - The national peacock dances in the rain

The peacock is India's national bird, famous for its majestic dance in the rain. During showers, the peacock unfurls its magnificent feathers, forming a fan of glittering colors, to perform an impressive dance. This dance is not just a spectacle for the human eye, it's part of the male's seduction ritual. Male peacocks dance to attract the attention of females, using rain as a natural trigger to display their feathers in all their splendor.

Peacock feathers, with their reflections of green, blue and gold, are particularly prized for their beauty. In India, they often symbolize prosperity and benevolence. The peacock dance is said to herald rain, and in many rural areas, people watch this dance with some anticipation, as it often heralds the coming of the monsoon. This link between the peacock and rain reinforces its special place in the Indian imagination, where the bird is often depicted in scenes of lush nature.

The peacock also plays an important role in Indian mythology. It is associated with several Hindu gods, including the goddess Sarasvati, who represents wisdom, and the god Kartikeya, whose vehicle is a peacock. This majestic bird often appears in sacred stories and religious paintings, adding to its aura of grandeur. This special status led India to declare the peacock a national bird in 1963, reinforcing its link with Indian culture and nature.

Peacocks live mainly in the forests and plains of India, where they are often seen in groups, moving about freely. Their plumage protects them from predators by allowing them to blend in with the surrounding vegetation, but it's their courtship that these birds are most famous for. The male, who wears the most beautiful plumage, puts himself forward to impress the females, using a range of movements to make his feathers even more visible.

The beauty of the peacock and its dance in the rain are symbols not only of Indian nature, but also of the country's rich biodiversity. In India, monsoon rains are vital for agriculture, and to see a peacock unfurling its feathers at such times is seen as a sign of good fortune. Its image, linked to fertility and abundance, makes it a bird as respected as it is admired throughout the country.

Fact 4 - The Rewa white tiger is extremely rare

The Rewa white tiger is one of the rarest and most fascinating creatures in the animal world. Contrary to what you might think, it is not a different species of tiger, but a very rare genetic variant of the Bengal tiger. Its white color is not due to albinism, but to a genetic mutation called leucism, which depigments its coat while maintaining the black stripes characteristic of tigers. The white tiger's eyes, often blue, add to its extraordinary appearance.

The first known white tiger was discovered in 1951 in the Rewa region of India's Madhya Pradesh state. This tiger, named Mohan, was captured by the Maharaja of Rewa, who was fascinated by the animal's unique beauty. Mohan was then used to develop a line of white tigers in captivity, but in the wild, these animals remain extremely rare. Their rarity is partly explained by the difficulty they face in surviving in the wild. Their white coat makes them more visible to prey, and therefore harder to hide in the forests where tigers usually live.

Although many white tigers now live in captivity, notably in zoos and reserves, their appearance in the wild is virtually non-existent. Most of the white tigers we see are the result of breeding between individuals selected to maintain this genetic characteristic. However, in their natural environment, survival is extremely difficult. Nature prefers tigers with orange coats, better adapted to their environment.

The Rewa white tiger has also left its mark on Indian history and culture. For decades, it symbolized royalty and power in this region. The maharajas of Rewa considered the tiger a national treasure. Even today, the town of Rewa is proud to be the birthplace of the first known white tiger, and it has become something of an emblem for the region, attracting visitors fascinated by this rarity.

The protection of tigers, both white and non-white, remains a major issue in India. Thanks to conservation efforts, the tiger population has gradually increased in some reserves. The white tiger, though a curiosity of nature, is a reminder of the importance of protecting tiger habitat to safeguard their long-term survival.

Fact 5 - The Deccan Plateau, one of the world's oldest formations

The Deccan Plateau, located in central and southern India, is one of the oldest geological formations on the planet. This vast plateau of over 1.5 million square kilometers stretches from central India to the Western and Eastern Ghats. Its origins date back hundreds of millions of years, to a time when Pangea, the single supercontinent, was splitting up. The soil of the Deccan is mainly composed of basalt, a volcanic rock formed by lava flows that covered the region some 65 million years ago.

The Deccan Plateau is also known for its famous Deccan Trapps, rock formations resulting from gigantic volcanic eruptions that took place at the end of the dinosaur era. These massive eruptions covered the region with successive layers of lava, creating a terraced structure. Some studies suggest that these eruptions may even have contributed to the extinction of the dinosaurs. Today, these formations give the region its unique relief, with hills, valleys and escarpments.

This plateau has played a key role in the history and development of Indian civilization. For centuries, it formed a natural barrier between northern and southern India, influencing cultural and commercial exchanges. Numerous dynasties have ruled this region, notably the Chalukyas and Marathas. The Deccan Plateau is also home to several important historic cities, such as Hyderabad, Pune and Bangalore, which continue to be major economic and cultural centers today.

The plateau's climate is marked by hot, dry summers and moderate monsoons. The region is also known for its mineral-rich soil, which is particularly well-suited to agriculture. The fertile, well-drained volcanic soils of the Deccan are ideal for growing cotton, sugarcane and spices. These natural resources have contributed to the region's rise as a thriving agricultural center since ancient times.

Beyond its historical and economic importance, the Deccan Plateau offers magnificent scenery, with its craggy rock formations, vast plains and seasonal waterways. Its unique ecosystems, such as dry forests and grasslands, are home to numerous species of flora and fauna. The Deccan Plateau is thus not only a fascinating geological relic, but also a living region that continues to influence daily life in India.

Fact 6 - The Spiti valley resembles a lunar landscape

Located in the Himalayas, the Spiti Valley is often compared to a lunar landscape. At over 3,800 meters above sea level, this desert region in the state of Himachal Pradesh offers an astonishing spectacle, with its vast arid expanses, rugged mountains and intense blue skies. The valley is characterized by rock formations that seem to have been sculpted by wind and time, giving the impression of being on another planet. Walking through these landscapes, you sometimes feel as if you're walking on the Moon, so austere and spectacular is the environment.

Spiti, which means "middle land" in Tibetan, is landlocked between Tibet and the rest of India, which explains its isolation and Tibetan cultural influences. The valley's extreme climate, with temperatures plunging well below zero in winter, also contributes to the impression of a lunar desert. In summer, the few streams that flow through the valley offer luminous reflections on the white and brown rocks, further accentuating the impression of a mineral world frozen in time.

The Spiti valley has been inhabited for centuries by Buddhist communities who have built impressive monasteries here. Key Monastery, perched on a hill at over 4,000 meters, is an emblematic example of local architecture, surrounded by an almost unreal setting. These monasteries, overlooking the valley, add a spiritual touch to this mineral landscape. They are not only places of worship, but also centers of learning for Buddhist monks, perpetuating age-old traditions in this remote location.

The villages dotted around the valley also seem to have stepped out of another world. The white houses, often built of adobe, blend perfectly into the arid environment. Due to the altitude and climatic conditions, the inhabitants live mainly from subsistence farming, growing cereals such as barley and cold-hardy vegetables. Life in the Spiti Valley is hard, but the inhabitants adapt to this harsh climate with admirable resilience.

The rugged beauty and isolation of the Spiti Valley make it a popular destination for trekking and adventure enthusiasts, but access is difficult. In winter, the region is completely cut off from the rest of the world by snow. Summer adventurers are rewarded with breathtaking scenery and immersion in a unique culture. It's a place where nature reigns supreme, shaping people's lives and the scenery that surrounds them.

Fact 7 - The Western Ghats, one of the world's oldest chains

The Western Ghats, a mountain range stretching over 1,600 kilometers along India's west coast, are among the oldest geological formations on the planet. These mountains date back millions of years, long before the Himalayas. Their origins date back to the time when tectonic plates shifted to form the Indian subcontinent. Today, the Western Ghats stand like a natural barrier between the Deccan Plateau and the Arabian Sea, playing a crucial role in India's climate and ecology.

One of the special features of the Western Ghats is their immense biodiversity. The region is recognized as one of the world's 36 biodiversity hotspots. More than 7,000 plant species grow here, of which around 1,700 are found nowhere else in the world. Among the animals that inhabit the range are elephants, tigers, leopards and even Asiatic lions in some parts. The Ghats are also home to a rich variety of birds, amphibians and insects, making them a favorite spot for scientists and naturalists.

These mountains also have a significant influence on the region's climate. By intercepting monsoon winds from the Arabian Sea, they generate heavy rainfall on their western slopes, creating dense tropical forests. It is this rain that feeds many rivers, including some of South India's most important, such as the Godavari and Krishna. On the other side of the Ghats, on the eastern slopes, the climate is drier, which explains the marked difference between the two slopes.

Historically, the Western Ghats have played an important role in India's culture and economy. The forests of this region have long been exploited for their resources, notably teak wood and bamboo. Ancient civilizations flourished here, and several important archaeological sites have been discovered in the region. Today, the mountains are home to plantations of tea, coffee and spices such as pepper and cardamom, which are exported worldwide.

The Western Ghats are also a place of unsurpassed natural beauty. Landscapes range from lush green hills to sheer cliffs and impressive waterfalls. Among the most famous are the Jog Falls, the highest in India. The region attracts hikers, nature lovers and photographers, who come to capture the splendor of this thousand-year-old mountain range. The Western Ghats are therefore not only a geological marvel, but also an ecological and cultural treasure trove for India.

Fact 8 - The concept of mathematical infinity has roots in India

The concept of infinity, which has intrigued mathematicians for millennia, has deep roots in Indian thought. As early as the 5th century, mathematical and philosophical texts in India explored the idea of infinity in various forms, long before the concept was formalized in Europe. The Indian mathematician and astronomer Aryabhata, in his work on astronomy and mathematics, was one of the first to take an interest in notions linked to infinity, analyzing immense astronomical distances and endless cosmic cycles.

Ancient Hindu texts, particularly those in Sanskrit, already used specific terms to evoke infinity, such as "ananta", meaning "without end". This thinking was not confined to the pure sciences, but also permeated Indian philosophy. In the Rig Veda, one of the oldest sacred texts, there is frequent mention of an infinity of time and space, a concept that influenced the way Indian scholars and philosophers viewed the world. Mathematics and cosmology were therefore closely linked in ancient India.

Brahmagupta, another famous Indian mathematician of the 7th century, also contributed to the understanding of infinity in mathematics. He was one of the first to define precise rules for handling infinite quantities in his work. For example, he studied what happens when a number is divided by zero, leading to results that imply infinity. His contribution was decisive for the birth of algebra, and inspired generations of mathematicians after him.

It was not until several centuries later that European mathematicians such as Georg Cantor took the concept of infinity a step further, developing it into set theory. However, the influence of Indian discoveries in this field is undeniable. The concepts developed by Indian mathematicians paved the way for a more formal understanding of infinity. Their ideas crossed frontiers, inspiring Arab thinkers before reaching Europe in the Middle Ages.

Infinity, which remains a subject of fascination for scientists and philosophers to this day, has a long and deep-rooted history in India. Whether through the study of mathematics or cosmology, Indian thinkers have helped transform an abstract notion into an idea central to the understanding of our universe. The exploration of infinity bears witness not only to the scientific progress of ancient India, but also to the depth of its philosophical thought.

Fact 9 - Golconde Fort, renowned for its acoustics

Golconde Fort, located near Hyderabad in the state of Telangana, is a jewel of Indian military architecture. Built in the 16th century, this imposing fort is known not only for its massive walls and granite structures, but also for its incredible acoustic system. Spanning eight kilometers, the fort was designed in such a way that even a faint sound could be heard from several hundred meters away. This engineering feat enhanced the fortress's security at a time when rapid communication was vital.

One of the most fascinating features of Golconde Fort is that a simple clap of the hands at the main gate can be heard all the way to the top of the fort, more than a kilometer away. This ingenious acoustic system served to warn the guards of an attack, enabling them to react quickly. This sound transmission system, based on physical principles such as sound reflection, demonstrates just how expert the builders of the time were in acoustics, without having access to modern technology.

Surrounded by thick walls and punctuated by bastions, the fort also housed a palace complex, temples and underground cisterns, proving that Golconde was not just a fortification, but a real walled city. At the top of the fort, the citadel offered an unobstructed view of the surrounding area, allowing surveillance to detect any threat. The structure itself was designed to allow sound to propagate easily, an impressive architectural feat for its time.

Golconde also has a special place in Indian diamond history. The area around the fort was once famous for its diamond mines, and some of the world's most famous stones, such as Koh-i-Noor and Hope, are said to have been discovered nearby. This wealth enabled the kingdom of Golconde to prosper for centuries, attracting merchants and adventurers from far and wide to acquire these precious gems.

Today, Golconde Fort is a major tourist attraction. Visitors come not only to admire the fort's architectural ingenuity and panoramic views, but also to experience first-hand its famous acoustics. Just clap your hands at the entrance to feel this direct link with the past, a unique way to perceive the technical and cultural wealth of ancient India.

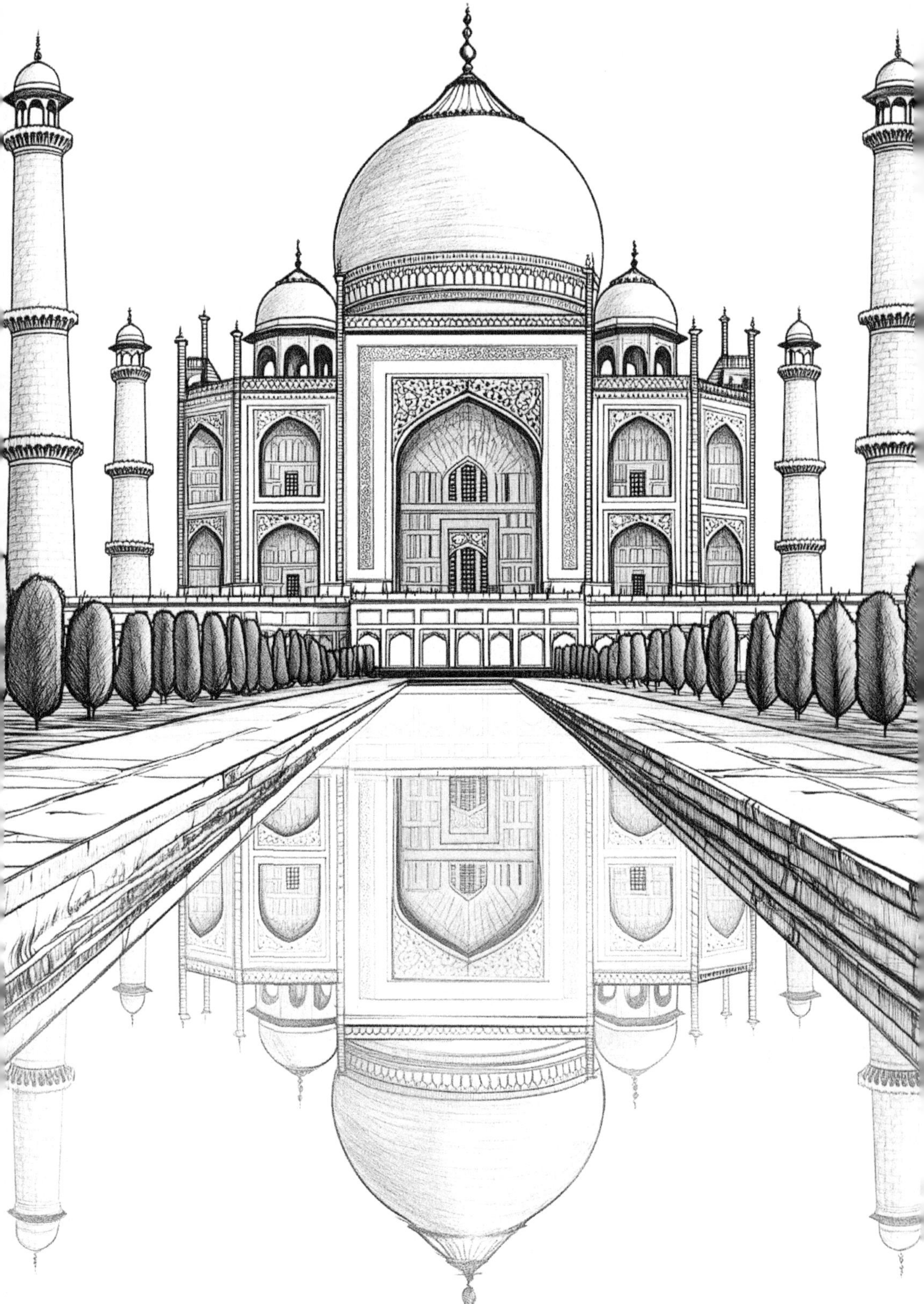

Fact 10 - The Taj Mahal changes color with the light

The Taj Mahal, one of the world's most famous monuments, is often described as a masterpiece of Mughal architecture. Built of white marble, this mausoleum is not only impressive for its size and symmetry, but also for its ability to change color according to the light of day. At dawn, the Taj Mahal takes on a delicate pink hue. During the day, it glows brilliantly white in direct sunlight, and at sunset, it turns golden before taking on a bluish hue in the light of the moon.

This color change is due to the particular quality of the marble used in its construction. This marble, extracted from the Makrana quarries in Rajasthan, is of exceptional purity. It reflects light in a unique way, capturing the nuances of the sky and surrounding shadows. This phenomenon is not only a spectacular visual effect, but also reinforces the mystical aura surrounding the Taj Mahal. Many visitors return at different times of the day to observe these transformations and admire the monument from different light angles.

The choice of white marble and changing light also has symbolic significance. The Taj Mahal, built by Emperor Shah Jahan in memory of his late wife Mumtaz Mahal, embodies eternal love and mourning. Variations in color, evoking the cycle of day and night, reflect the changing nature of life and death. For Shah Jahan, the Taj was intended not only as a resting place for his beloved, but also as a poetic representation of the immortality of their love.

The architecture of the Taj Mahal, with its imposing domes and elegant minarets, further accentuates this color-changing effect. The large pool in front of the mausoleum, which reflects the image of the Taj, also plays a part in this visual illusion. At sunrise or dusk, visitors can observe the Taj Mahal's inverted image in the water, creating a perfect symmetry that amplifies the monument's changing beauty.

The Taj Mahal continues to attract millions of visitors every year, not only for its architecture and moving history, but also for the visual magic that makes it a living monument, changing with the passage of time. Those lucky enough to see it under the light of a full moon often testify to its unique, almost surreal atmosphere, where the marble seems to glow with a soft, mysterious light. The Taj Mahal is thus more than just a mausoleum; it is a moving work of art, capturing the nuances of light and time.

Fact 11 - The Chambal River is home to rare crocodiles

The Chambal River, which flows through the states of Rajasthan, Madhya Pradesh and Uttar Pradesh, is one of the last natural refuges for rare crocodile species, including the gharial. This long-snouted reptile, unique for its tapered shape, is a critically endangered species. The Chambal is one of the few rivers where it is still possible to observe them in their natural habitat, far from the human pressures that have reduced their numbers in other parts of India.

The gharial, which can grow up to six meters long, is a fishing specialist. Its long, narrow snout and sharp teeth enable it to catch fish with great efficiency. Unlike other crocodiles, it almost never attacks humans, as its diet consists almost exclusively of fish. The Chambal River, with its clear waters and unspoilt banks, provides an ideal environment for these silent predators, which often glide through the water without a sound, invisible to the naked eye.

In addition to the gharial, Chambal is also home to another rare species: the marsh crocodile, also known as the mugger. This crocodile, more robust than the gharial, is also endangered, though less critically so. Conservation efforts around the river have enabled both species to survive, despite the progressive destruction of their habitat in other parts of the country. The Chambal National Sanctuary, created in 1979, protects over 400 kilometers of the river, providing a safe haven for these creatures as well as many other species.

The Chambal River is also home to rare river dolphins and aquatic turtles, creating an incredibly diverse ecosystem. This unique biodiversity is one of the reasons why the Chambal remains relatively wild and untouched by human industry. Travelers who venture to this region can observe these endangered species at close quarters, especially during boat trips along the river, a privileged way to admire these animals in their natural environment.

Long associated with tales of bandits who once prowled the region, the Chambal River today hides another treasure: a rich and precious biodiversity that it is essential to protect. The rare crocodiles of the Chambal have become a symbol of the struggle to preserve river ecosystems in India, and their survival depends entirely on continued efforts to preserve this exceptional environment.

Fact 12 - Diwali lights up the whole of India every year

Diwali, often called the Festival of Lights, is celebrated with fervor throughout India every year, marking one of the most important events in the Hindu calendar. The festival symbolizes the victory of light over darkness, of good over evil, and is celebrated by millions of families. During this period, houses, temples and even streets are decorated with rows of oil lamps, called diyas, which glow throughout the night. These little flames represent hope, prosperity and the triumph of spiritual light over inner darkness.

Diwali has its origins in Hindu mythology. The story most commonly associated with this festival tells of King Rama's triumphant return to Ayodhya after fourteen years of exile and after defeating the demon Ravana. To welcome Rama, the people of Ayodhya lit rows of lamps, illuminating the city in a show of joy and welcome. Even today, this gesture is repeated throughout the country, with each lighted lamp symbolizing the celebration of this victorious return.

Although Diwali is primarily a Hindu festival, it is also celebrated by other communities in India. Jains, for example, commemorate the nirvana of Lord Mahavira, while for Sikhs, Diwali marks the release of the sixth Guru, Guru Hargobind, from captivity. This makes Diwali a multicultural festival, where religious beliefs come together in a common celebration. In addition to diyas, fireworks light up the sky on Diwali night, symbolizing the explosion of joy and triumph.

Beyond its spiritual dimension, Diwali is also a time for family sharing. Families come together to exchange gifts, enjoy traditional dishes and sweets prepared especially for the occasion. Local markets fill up with garlands of lights, colorful decorations and sweets like ladoo and barfi, which are shared among neighbors and friends. Homes are carefully cleaned and decorated, as it is believed that the goddess Lakshmi, goddess of prosperity, visits homes during Diwali to bring luck and happiness.

This festival of lights unites the whole of India in a burst of color, light and festivity. Whether celebrated in large metropolises like Mumbai or in small villages, Diwali transcends social and cultural differences, offering a moment of peace, brotherhood and hope. This festival, which literally lights up the country, reminds everyone of the importance of light, not only in the physical world, but also in the heart and mind of each individual.

Fact 13 - The Brahmaputra passes through three countries

The Brahmaputra, one of Asia's greatest rivers, is remarkable not only for its size and power, but also for the fact that it flows through three different countries: China, India and Bangladesh. It rises on the Tibetan plateau at an altitude of around 5,300 metres, under the name of Yarlung Tsangpo. The sacred river then winds its way for almost 2,900 kilometers through mountainous landscapes before entering India, where it changes face and becomes the Brahmaputra.

Crossing the state of Arunachal Pradesh, then Assam, the Brahmaputra becomes a powerful river, essential to the economy and daily life of the millions of people who live on its banks. It feeds vast fertile plains, which are ideal for agriculture, particularly the cultivation of rice and tea, the region's emblematic products. The river is also a valuable source of fish and serves as a transportation route for goods and passengers.

One of the special features of the Brahmaputra is its unpredictable behavior. During the monsoon season, its waters swell considerably, causing spectacular flooding, particularly on the Assam plain. Although devastating, these floods also provide essential nutrients for agricultural soils. However, rising water levels require considerable protective measures for riverside populations, who must constantly adapt their homes and crops to the river's vagaries.

In Bangladesh, where the Brahmaputra joins the Ganges to form the Sundarbans delta, it takes on even greater importance. This delta, the largest in the world, is a region rich in biodiversity, home to mangroves and rare species such as the Bengal tiger. The river and its tributaries shape and feed this vast region, making the Brahmaputra one of the vital arteries of the South Asian ecosystem.

The Brahmaputra is not only a geographical wonder, but also a cultural and spiritual symbol for many communities in India and beyond. It is revered as a sacred river, bringing life and fertility. Its importance transcends political boundaries, uniting three nations through its mighty waters, while connecting millions of people across its majestic course.

Fact 14 - India's parliament sits in a circular building

The Indian Parliament, located in New Delhi, sits in a building that is unique in its form: a huge circular edifice that symbolizes unity and inclusion. Known as the Sansad Bhavan, the building was designed by British architects Edwin Lutyens and Herbert Baker in the 1920s, during the colonial period. Its circular shape, unusually rare for a legislative building, evokes a perfect circle, suggesting the idea of equality and unity among the nation's representatives, with no end and no beginning, where everyone has a role to play.

The building is a masterpiece of Indo-British architecture. It measures around 170 meters in diameter and is surrounded by 144 massive sandstone columns, giving it a majestic appearance. The heart of the parliament is the central hall, where the joint sessions of the two chambers are held: the Lok Sabha (House of the People) and the Rajya Sabha (Council of States). This circular design allows legislators to debate in an open, symbolically inclusive space, where all voices, from north to south, east to west, are expected to meet.

The importance of the circular shape doesn't stop there. The Sansad Bhavan is also a fascinating example of adaptation to local culture. Its design takes into account the principles of Vastu Shastra, an ancient Indian science of architecture, to align the building's positive energies. The building is surrounded by lush gardens, and its massive red sandstone structure is inspired by the architectural styles of Indian palaces, making it both monumental and rooted in India's cultural heritage.

It is in this iconic building that key decisions are made, shaping the future of the world's largest democracy. The debates that take place within its walls influence the lives of over 1.3 billion people, making the Sansad Bhavan one of the world's most important political centers. It was here that crucial legislation was passed, including the Indian Constitution in 1950, marking the beginning of the Indian Republic.

Today, although the Sansad Bhavan is a powerful symbol of Indian democracy, the country's growth has necessitated the construction of a new, modern parliamentary complex nearby, to better meet the needs of the country's expanding population. However, the original circular building remains deeply etched in Indian history as a symbol of inclusiveness and democratic continuity.

Fact 15 - Ghee, the clarified butter essential to Indian cuisine

Ghee, or clarified butter, is one of the most essential and ancient ingredients in Indian cuisine. It is prepared by melting butter to remove impurities and water, leaving only pure, golden fats. This process gives ghee a smooth texture and a unique nutty taste, which is prized for its rich flavor and culinary versatility. Used in a multitude of dishes, from curries to desserts, ghee adds a depth of flavor that sets it apart from other fats.

In Indian tradition, ghee is regarded not only as a food, but also as a sacred ingredient. It is used in religious rituals, where it is burned in lamps or offered to deities during ceremonies. The symbolism of ghee dates back to ancient texts such as the Vedas, which describe it as pure and nourishing for body and soul. Even today, it is often used in traditional celebrations, reinforcing its cultural importance in addition to its culinary uses.

Nutritionally, ghee is also respected for its many benefits. It is rich in short-chain saturated fatty acids, which facilitate digestion and help absorb fat-soluble vitamins such as A, D, E and K. According to Ayurveda, the traditional Indian medicine, ghee is renowned for its healing properties, believed to stimulate the digestive system and boost immunity. What's more, it is often preferred to vegetable oils for high-temperature cooking, as it does not break down easily, thus preserving its benefits.

Ghee is ubiquitous in the cuisines of all regions of India. Whether coating rotis or chapatis with a thin layer of melting ghee or incorporating it into a steaming dal tadka, it is a fundamental ingredient in many dishes. Desserts such as halwa or ladoo are also prepared with ghee, which gives them a rich, melt-in-the-mouth texture. This universal use of ghee in Indian cuisine makes it an irreplaceable ingredient.

The Indian love affair with ghee extends beyond the kitchen. In many families, it is made at home from fresh milk, perpetuating an ancient tradition. The process of making ghee, though simple, is often seen as an act of care and generosity. This attachment to ghee shows that this ingredient is much more than a simple fat: it embodies history, culture and health in the daily lives of Indians.

Fact 16 - The Kumbh Mela brings together 100 million people

The Kumbh Mela is the world's largest religious gathering, attracting millions of pilgrims, saints, sadhus and visitors from all over India and beyond. This Hindu festival is held every 12 years, alternating between four sacred sites: Allahabad (Prayagraj), Haridwar, Nashik and Ujjain. At the 2013 edition in Allahabad, the Kumbh Mela broke records with over 100 million participants. This colossal figure testifies to the religious fervor that surrounds this age-old event, deeply rooted in Indian culture.

The Kumbh Mela is centered around a particular ritual: the purifying bath in a sacred river. It is believed that bathing in these waters during the Kumbh erases sins and helps progress on the spiritual path. The rivers where the Kumbh takes place, such as the Ganges in Haridwar or the Triveni Sangam (the confluence of the Ganges, the Yamuna and the mythical Sarasvati) in Allahabad, are considered particularly conducive to this spiritual purification. The key moments of the Kumbh, known as Shahi Snan, see huge crowds rush into the water at sunrise.

This spiritual gathering is rooted in Hindu mythology. Legend tells of a cosmic battle between the gods (devas) and demons (asuras) for immortality. During this battle, four drops of divine nectar (amrita) fell to Earth, marking the four cities where the Kumbh Mela is celebrated. This mythological event is at the heart of the festivities, and each Kumbh is an opportunity to reconnect with this sacred history, the importance of which has been handed down from generation to generation.

In addition to the religious aspect, the Kumbh Mela is a time of unparalleled social and cultural gathering. Ashrams, temporary camps and markets spring up in the host cities, creating a vibrant ephemeral city. Pilgrims come not only to bathe, but also to meet holy men, listen to spiritual discourses and take part in age-old rituals. Although rooted in Hinduism, the event also attracts many curious onlookers and spiritual seekers from all over the world, fascinated by the scale and intensity of the devotion.

The logistics of such a gigantic event are impressive. Local authorities work months in advance to ensure security, manage temporary infrastructures, and organize the movement of millions of people. The fact that millions of pilgrims gather peacefully around a common spiritual goal testifies to the unity and diversity of India's faith. The Kumbh Mela, with its sheer scale and cultural depth, remains a unique event in the world.

Fact 17 - Monkeys protect temples in India

In India, monkeys, especially macaques and langurs, are more than just wild animals: they play a protective role in certain temples. This is particularly true in temples dedicated to Hanuman, the monkey god, who is revered for his strength, devotion and courage. Monkeys are often considered the natural guardians of these sacred places, roaming freely among pilgrims and visitors. In places like the Hanuman temple in Hampi or the Galta temple in Jaipur, monkeys are almost an integral part of spiritual life.

In these temples, monkeys are not only tolerated, but also respected. Believers regularly feed them with fruit and other foods, a gesture considered an act of piety. These animals, which roam freely in temple courtyards and gardens, in turn seem to protect the premises from intruders or unwanted visitors. There are many local accounts of how the monkeys are said to have "chased away" ill-intentioned people from temple grounds, reinforcing their image as divine protectors.

Macaques and langurs are not chosen for this sacred role by chance. In Hindu tradition, monkeys are associated with Hanuman, a mythological character known for his loyalty to the god Rama and his exploits in the epic Ramayana. Hanuman, with his legendary strength and wisdom, is often portrayed as a model of courage and loyalty. Monkeys, by being associated with this figure, embody these same values and are therefore treated with great respect in these religious places.

However, their presence can sometimes cause challenges for temple managers and visitors alike. Curious and bold, these monkeys don't mind stealing food or personal items, adding a touch of unpredictability to temple visits. Yet even in the face of such mischievous behavior, most devotees regard them as manifestations of Hanuman's spirit, accepting these little "mishaps" with indulgence.

These temples, where monkeys are both revered and feared, offer a fascinating interaction between man, nature and the sacred. The monkeys occupy a unique place, halfway between the wild and spiritual worlds, a constant reminder of the fragile, respectful balance that Indians maintain with their environment and their beliefs. It is this living, dynamic aspect of the temples, where the animal plays an active role, that makes these places extraordinary examples of spiritual and natural coexistence.

Fact 18 - Delhi's Red Fort, witness to the Mughal emperors

Delhi's Red Fort, also known as Lal Qila, is an imposing historical monument that was the seat of power for the Mughal emperors for over two centuries. Built by Emperor Shah Jahan in 1638, the fort takes its name from the distinctive color of its red sandstone walls. Situated in the heart of the Indian capital, it still bears witness to the grandeur and power of the Mughal Empire, which left a lasting imprint on India's history. The fort is a spectacular example of Indo-Islamic architecture, blending Persian, Timurid and Indian influences.

Not only is the Red Fort an architectural masterpiece, it has also played a key role in India's political history. It was from its ramparts that Prime Minister Jawaharlal Nehru delivered India's independence speech in 1947. Every year since, on August 15, Independence Day, the Prime Minister climbs the ramparts of the fort to address the nation. This tradition reinforces the symbolic importance of the Red Fort as a witness to India's transition from British colonial rule to an independent republic.

The Red Fort was once home to the imperial Mughal court, with its palaces, pavilions and lush gardens. Among the most famous buildings inside the fort are the Diwan-i-Aam, the public audience hall, where the emperor dispensed justice to his subjects. There's also the Diwan-i-Khas, the private audience hall, decorated with marble and jewels, where the emperor received foreign dignitaries and guests. These rooms recall the wealth and refinement of the Mughal court, where art and architecture were at the service of imperial power.

However, the history of the Red Fort is not limited to Mughal splendor. In the 19th century, following the Indian revolt of 1857 against British rule, the last Mughal emperor, Bahadur Shah Zafar, was imprisoned in this very fort before being exiled to Burma. This was a decisive turning point in Indian history, marking the end of the mighty Mughal Empire. The Red Fort is thus a place where India's glorious and tragic memories intersect, reflecting the struggles and triumphs of this vast country.

Today, Delhi's Red Fort is a UNESCO World Heritage Site and a must-see destination for visitors from all over the world. It remains a vibrant symbol of India's Mughal heritage and freedom struggle. Visitors strolling through its vast courtyards and marble pavilions can still feel the echo of the past and the historical significance of this unique monument, which has survived the centuries by remaining at the heart of Indian history.

Fact 19 - The bhut jolokia pepper is one of the strongest

Bhut jolokia, sometimes called "ghost pepper", is one of the world's most powerful chillies. Grown mainly in the northeastern states of India, such as Assam, Nagaland and Manipur, this pepper is so strong that it has long held the record for the hottest pepper on the Scoville scale. With a scale reaching over a million Scoville units, bhut jolokia is over 400 times hotter than jalapeño. This extreme intensity has made it a culinary curiosity, but also an ingredient used with great care.

The name bhut jolokia means "ghost pepper", a nickname that evokes its lightning effect on the taste buds. It's so potent that cooks often add just a tiny amount to dishes, just enough to give them a kick of heat without making them inedible. In Assam, it is used to spice up curries and chutneys, but always sparingly. Some locals eat chillies raw, but it's a real challenge that only a handful of people are capable of meeting.

Bhut jolokia is also used in contexts that go beyond cooking. Because of its intense heat, some rural communities use it as a natural repellent against wild elephants. Fences coated with chili paste or tear-gas grenades made from bhut jolokia have been tested to keep these animals away from villages and crops. This use illustrates just how powerful and feared this chilli is, even by the largest animals.

Despite its extreme spiciness, bhut jolokia has a number of health benefits. Like many hot peppers, it is rich in capsaicin, a chemical compound responsible for the burning sensation, but also known for its analgesic and anti-inflammatory properties. In traditional medicine, bhut jolokia is used to relieve pain, improve blood circulation and even boost metabolism.

Today, the bhut jolokia continues to fascinate thrill-seekers and culinary researchers the world over. Although it has been dethroned by even stronger varieties, it remains a symbol of the power of Indian chillies. Its popularity is even growing internationally, where it is used in ultra-hot sauces and tasting competitions, testing the mettle of those who dare to try it.

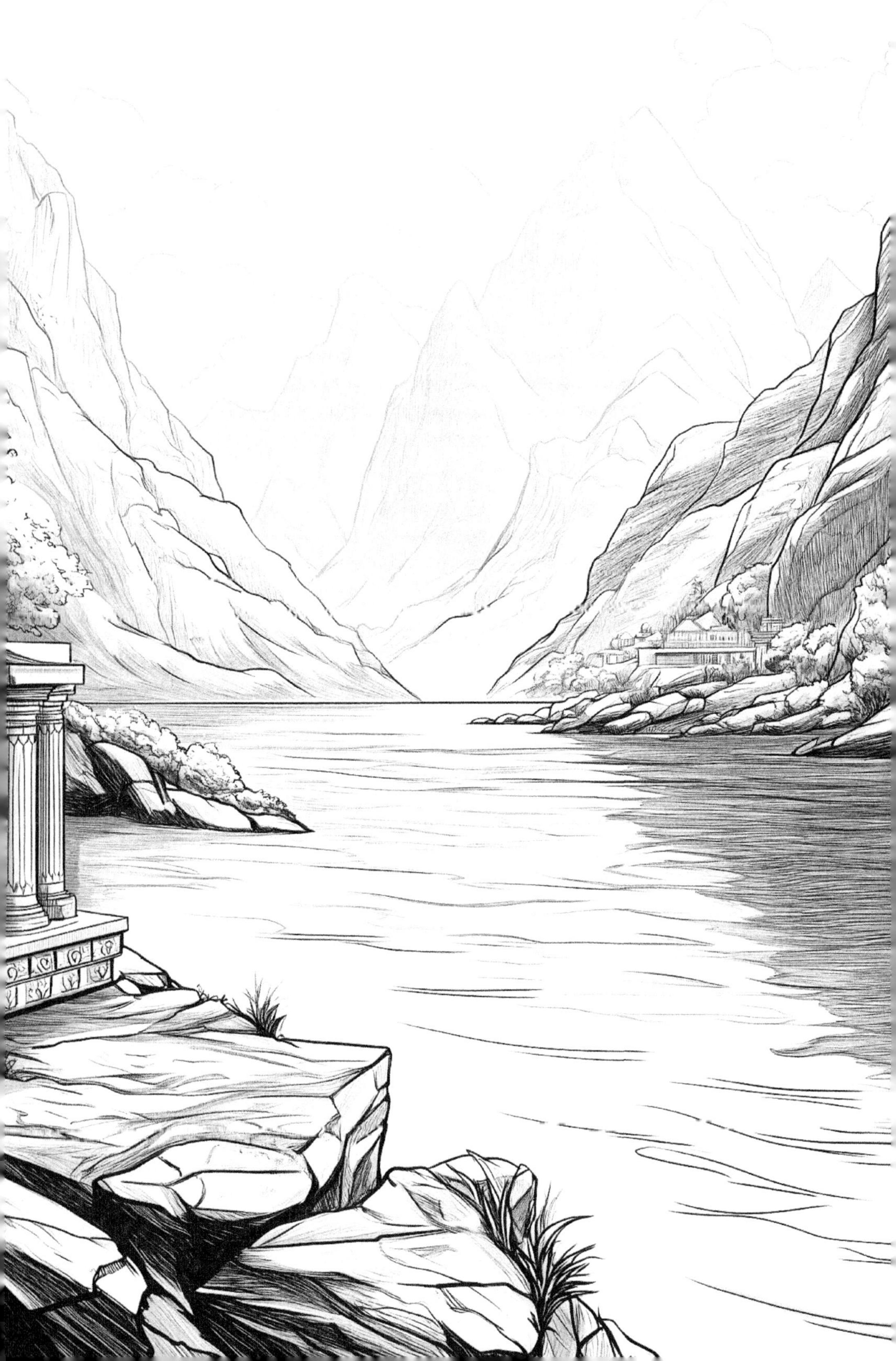

Fact 20 - The Sarasvati, India's mythical vanishing river

The Sarasvati is one of the most famous and mysterious rivers of ancient India. Mentioned in the sacred texts of the Rig Veda, it was once described as a powerful and majestic river, nurturing the civilizations that flourished on its banks. However, unlike other sacred rivers such as the Ganges or the Yamuna, the Sarasvati disappeared from the earth's surface thousands of years ago, leading to much speculation about its existence and exact course.

According to ancient scriptures, the Sarasvati was an immense river, flowing from the Himalayan mountains to the Arabian Sea. It would have fed some of India's earliest civilizations, notably the Indus Valley civilization. However, geologists and historians believe that climatic changes and tectonic movements may have dried up its bed, diverting its waters to other rivers, or forcing it to become an underground river. This disappearance has given the Sarasvati an almost mythical status, transforming it into an invisible sacred river.

Today, Sarasvati is worshipped not only as a river, but also as a goddess of wisdom, the arts and knowledge. In Hinduism, the goddess Sarasvati is depicted holding a veena (musical instrument) and sitting on a lotus. She symbolizes purity of thought and speech. Although her physical course is no longer visible, her presence in Indian spirituality remains alive, and she is often invoked in prayers for learning and intellectual success.

Modern archaeological and geological research has attempted to retrace the course of this vanished river. Satellite images and field studies have revealed fossilized underground river beds in north-west India, possibly corresponding to the ancient bed of the Sarasvati. These discoveries continue to fascinate researchers, as they may not only shed light on the past, but also offer clues to the ancient Indian civilizations that depended on this river for their survival.

The Sarasvati, despite her physical demise, occupies a central place in India's collective imagination. Its myth is a reminder of the importance of rivers not only as sources of water, but also as symbols of life and culture. It remains a link between ancient and modern India, where the quest to find this sunken river reflects the desire to understand and honor the deep roots of Indian civilization.

Fact 21 - Patanjali codified yoga millennia ago

Yoga, today's world-renowned spiritual and physical practice, has its roots in the teachings of Patanjali, an Indian sage who lived over 2,000 years ago. Patanjali is often credited with codifying yoga in the form of an essential text, the Yoga Sutras, which synthesize and organize ancient spiritual and philosophical practices. Although yoga existed long before him in various forms, it was Patanjali who gave the discipline a clear structure and made it accessible to millions of practitioners.

Patanjali's Yoga Sutras, written in 196 aphorisms, explain the purpose of yoga: to achieve a state of mental clarity and inner peace. These aphorisms cover a wide variety of aspects of yoga, from meditation and breathing techniques (pranayama), to physical postures (asanas), ethics and mastery of the senses. Patanjali described yoga as a path of eight stages, or ashtanga yoga, each designed to guide the individual towards spiritual awakening and liberation.

What sets Patanjali apart is his ability to structure yoga into a discipline that is accessible and applicable to everyday life. Unlike a simple series of physical exercises, yoga according to Patanjali is a complete system of spiritual development. He emphasized self-mastery, meditation and thought control as essential elements in achieving union between mind, body and soul. In this way, yoga becomes not only a physical practice, but also a means of achieving mental and emotional balance.

Beyond India, Patanjali's teachings have crossed the centuries and spread throughout the world. Today, millions of people practice yoga, from physical postures to meditation, often without even knowing that the foundations of this discipline can be traced back to the Yoga Sutras. The fact that these texts are still studied and followed shows just how timeless and universal Patanjali's wisdom remains, far beyond geographical and cultural boundaries.

Thanks to Patanjali, yoga has evolved into a universal practice that guides individuals towards physical and mental well-being. In India, he is revered as one of the greatest sages to have contributed to the country's culture and spirituality. The concepts he introduced continue to influence not only Indian philosophy, but also the way of life of many people around the world, making him a central figure in the history of yoga.

Fact 22 - The Sundarbans are home to unique swimming tigers

The Sundarbans, a vast mangrove delta on the border between India and Bangladesh, is home to a unique population of Bengal tigers. What sets them apart from their fellow tigers is their incredible ability to swim. Indeed, these tigers are seasoned swimmers, capable of crossing large expanses of salt water, a rare characteristic among felines. Living in an ecosystem where the mainland is interspersed with rivers and canals, they have developed this ability to move and hunt through their inhospitable habitat.

The ability of these tigers to swim is not only an impressive adaptation, it's also a necessity. The Sundarbans form one of the world's largest mangrove systems, a challenging environment where tides constantly change the landscape. To survive and expand their territory, tigers not only have to hunt deer and wild boar in the forests, but also have to be able to move through murky and sometimes deep waters. This ability to swim long distances is a true testament to their incredible adaptability.

Sundarbans tigers are also particularly notorious for their aggression and reputation as man-hunters, a fact made all the more apparent by their restricted habitat. The scarcity of prey and the difficulty of the terrain sometimes lead them to venture close to human habitations, reinforcing their status as both feared and respected creatures. The locals regard these tigers as both sacred and dangerous, and rituals are often performed to appease them and keep them at bay.

The relationship between tigers and mangroves is also crucial to the preservation of this ecosystem. Bengal tigers act as predators at the top of the food chain, regulating prey populations and maintaining the ecological balance of the Sundarbans. The preservation of these swimming tigers has become a priority for conservation efforts in India, as their disappearance would have dramatic consequences for the region's biodiversity.

The existence of the swimming tigers of the Sundarbans is a striking example of how wildlife can adapt to unique environments. These tigers, both majestic and powerful, are a testament to nature's resilience and the need to protect habitats as extraordinary as the Sundarbans. Their ability to swim and survive in these extreme conditions fascinates and inspires researchers and nature lovers the world over.

Fact 23 - Mehrangarh fort has remained impregnable for centuries

Perched 122 meters above the city of Jodhpur, Mehrangarh Fort is one of India's most imposing and impregnable fortresses. Built in the mid-15th century by Rao Jodha, the founder of Jodhpur, this massive fort has withstood the test of time and numerous attacks without ever being taken. Its gigantic ramparts, up to 36 meters high and 21 meters thick, make it a symbol of power and unshakeable defense. No enemy has ever succeeded in breaching its gates or defenses, giving it a legendary reputation.

The architecture of Mehrangarh Fort is impressive not only for its size, but also for its sophisticated engineering. Its massive gates, some with spikes to prevent war elephants from breaking through, and well-positioned watchtowers show just how well the fortress was designed to withstand attack. Every aspect of its construction, from solid walls to narrow passageways, has been designed to counter invasion attempts, making the fort virtually impregnable.

Mehrangarh Fort is not only a military fortress, it's also a veritable architectural and cultural treasure trove. Within its walls are several sumptuously decorated palaces, such as the Moti Mahal (Pearl Palace) and the Phool Mahal (Palace of Flowers), which bear witness to the wealth and elegance of the Rajput rulers. These palaces are adorned with magnificent frescoes, delicate carvings and latticed windows, recalling the splendor of Rajasthan's royal courts in medieval times.

Over the centuries, the fort not only served as the residence of Rajput kings, but also became an important cultural center. Today, Mehrangarh Fort houses a museum displaying precious artifacts, including ancient weapons, royal palanquins and miniature paintings. Considered one of the finest in India, the museum allows visitors to delve into the fascinating history of the region and appreciate the legacy of the Rajput dynasties that ruled Jodhpur.

With its ramparts overlooking the blue city of Jodhpur, Mehrangarh embodies a unique combination of military strength and architectural beauty. The panoramic view it affords over the arid landscapes of Rajasthan adds to its majesty. After centuries of existence, Mehrangarh Fort continues to be a source of local pride and a powerful testament to the human ability to build monuments that defy the test of time.

Fact 24 - The Indian elephant is sacred in Hinduism

The Indian elephant occupies a central place in Hinduism, where it is revered as a symbol of strength, wisdom and prosperity. This cultural and religious importance is particularly evident in the god Ganesh, one of the most popular deities in the Hindu pantheon, who is depicted with an elephant's head. Ganesh is the god who removes obstacles and is often invoked at the start of any undertaking or ritual. The figure of the elephant, associated with wisdom and good fortune, is also found in Hindu prayers and ceremonies.

Elephants are also present in Hindu temples throughout India. They are sometimes used in large religious processions, such as the Ganesh Chaturthi festival, where statues of Ganesh are carried around in great splendor. Some temples, such as the famous Guruvayur temple in the state of Kerala, even house elephants, which are considered sacred animals. These elephants take part in rituals and are cared for with the utmost devotion, symbolizing the divine presence on Earth.

In Hindu mythology, the elephant is also linked to the god Indra, king of the heavens, whose mount is Airavata, a majestic, multi-headed white elephant. This mythical elephant is said to bring rain and fertilize the earth, reinforcing the idea that the elephant is a protective and beneficent creature. This link between the elephant and the forces of nature shows just how deeply rooted this animal is in Indian beliefs and spiritual stories.

Religion aside, elephants also play an important role in Indian culture. Traditionally, elephants were used by kings and emperors in battle or to display their power and wealth. Maharajas decorated them with rich finery for official ceremonies, reinforcing their royal and sacred status. Today, this tradition lives on in festivals such as the one in Jaipur, where elephants are decorated with colorful fabrics and jewels to celebrate their privileged place in Indian culture.

Throughout the country, the Indian elephant is respected not only for its physical strength, but also for its spiritual and symbolic role. It is seen as a wise guide, capable of leading people to prosperity and success. The deep attachment Indians have for this animal is reflected in the way it is treated and protected, both in religious sanctuaries and in the wild, where efforts are made to preserve this precious species.

Fact 25 - Holi, the world-famous festival of colors

Holi, celebrated every year in spring, is one of India's most joyous and colorful festivals. It's also known as the "festival of colors", because it's accompanied by the unique tradition of throwing colored powders, called gulal, into the air and onto other participants. This explosion of color symbolizes the triumph of good over evil, as well as the arrival of spring and the renewal of nature. All over India, people gather to dance, sing and cover themselves in vibrant colors, making Holi a spectacular and vibrant event.

The origins of Holi can be traced back to mythological tales. The most popular story connected with the festival is that of Prahlad, a young devotee of the god Vishnu, who miraculously escaped from his demonic aunt, Holika, who had tried to kill him in a fire. This act of survival is celebrated every year with bonfires lit on the eve of Holi, during the Holika Dahan ceremony, symbolizing the victory of devotion and virtue over malevolence. This sacred tradition is a reminder of the importance of faith and courage in Indian culture.

This festival is also marked by the celebration of love and joy, particularly through the story of the god Krishna and his beloved Radha. Krishna, known for his playful spirit, is said to have used colored powders to dye the faces of Radha and her friends, an act which, according to legend, gave rise to the current custom of throwing colors. In Vrindavan and Mathura, places associated with Krishna, Holi is celebrated with particular intensity, attracting thousands of devotees and visitors.

Holi is not only a spiritual event, it's also a time of community celebration when all social and religious barriers are temporarily abolished. Men, women, rich or poor, everyone takes part in this collective burst of joy, sharing traditional foods such as gujiya and thandai, a refreshing drink. During this period, people visit each other, exchange good wishes, and spread an atmosphere of camaraderie and good cheer.

Although Holi is deeply rooted in Indian culture, it has now become a global phenomenon. Many countries now celebrate this colorful festival, attracting crowds from all over the world to take part in this moment of pure joy. Whether in India or abroad, Holi embodies the spirit of freedom, fraternity and renewal, a universal message that continues to resonate across cultures and generations.

Fact 26 - The dosa is a popular giant pancake

Dosa is a culinary specialty that originated in southern India, but its popularity now extends throughout the country. This thin, crispy pancake, made from fermented rice and black lentils, is cooked on a hot griddle to obtain a light, golden texture. The dosa can grow to an impressive size, sometimes over 30 centimeters in diameter, making it a giant pancake often rolled or folded before serving. It is usually accompanied by spicy chutneys and a bowl of sambar, a lentil and vegetable-based soup.

One of the most famous variations is masala dosa, stuffed with a spicy potato, onion and curry leaf preparation. This dish, which combines sweet and spicy flavors, is a favorite in tiffin restaurants specializing in South Indian breakfasts and snacks. Although light, dosa is extremely nourishing thanks to the protein provided by lentils and the energy of rice. It's perfect for starting the day or as a quick meal at any time.

Dosa is not just a dish, it's a culinary tradition handed down from generation to generation. Fermentation of the rice and lentil mixture is a key process, giving dosa its slightly tangy taste. Each family has its own method of preparation, and recipes may vary slightly from one region to another. This fermentation process, though simple, requires time and patience, making dosa not only delicious, but also rich in digestive benefits.

Although mainly associated with southern India, dosa has conquered the whole country, to the point of being ubiquitous on the menus of Indian restaurants, both modest and upscale. In town and country, dosa is a symbol of Indian hospitality. It is served at major events and religious festivals, and is often eaten in small street cafés called idli-dosa stalls, where it can be enjoyed fresh, cooked directly on a large griddle.

Today, dosa is one of the most recognized Indian dishes abroad. Restaurants specializing in Indian cuisine offer them in every corner of the globe, where this giant pancake continues to impress with its simplicity and diversity. Whether you're in India or elsewhere, savoring a dosa is to immerse yourself in one of the tastiest and most convivial traditions of Indian cuisine, a real treat for the taste buds.

Fact 27 - Thar welcomes camels adapted to arid conditions

The Thar Desert, also known as the Great Indian Desert, covers over 200,000 square kilometers, mainly in the state of Rajasthan. It is one of India's most arid regions, with high temperatures and little rainfall. Yet in this extreme climate, camels have not only survived, they have thrived. These animals, nicknamed "ships of the desert", are perfectly adapted to the arid conditions of the Thar and play an essential role in the lives of the local population.

The Thar camel, or dromedary camel, is particularly well equipped for the challenges of the desert. It can survive days without water, thanks to its unique ability to store fat in its hump, which is converted into energy when food or water are scarce. In addition to its ability to withstand the heat, its large hooves help it to walk on burning sands without sinking. This animal is also capable of drinking large quantities of water in a short space of time, up to 40 liters at a time, to compensate for long periods of dehydration.

The people of the Thar Desert depend heavily on camels for their survival. These animals are used as beasts of burden to transport goods, cross the dunes, and even pull carts in the villages. Camel milk is also an important source of nutrition for pastoral communities, while their wool is used to make clothing adapted to extreme climates. The Raika, a pastoral community specializing in camel breeding, play a key role in preserving this ancient relationship between man and camel.

The Pushkar Camel Festival, celebrated every year in Rajasthan, highlights the importance of these animals in local culture. The festival attracts thousands of visitors, who come to watch camel races, beauty contests and other shows featuring these majestic animals. The camel, with its elegance and robustness, is celebrated as a living symbol of adaptability and survival in one of India's harshest environments.

Today, although modernization has reduced the traditional use of camels in some areas, these animals remain indispensable to many aspects of daily life in the Thar Desert. Their cultural, economic and ecological importance continues to play a vital role in the sustainability of this region, demonstrating how people and animals coexist in a delicate balance in the heart of the desert.

Fact 28 - The Indian emblem inspired by Ashoka's lions

India's national emblem, found on all official documents and coins, is inspired by Ashoka's famous lion capital, one of the greatest symbols of India's historical and spiritual heritage. This capital, dating from the 3rd century B.C., stands in Sarnath, the place where Buddha is said to have given his first sermon after attaining enlightenment. Carved in polished sandstone, the capital features four majestic lions, turned back to back, representing strength, courage and unity.

Emperor Ashoka, who reigned over the Maurya Empire, was responsible for the creation of this emblematic monument. After converting to Buddhism, Ashoka adopted a policy of peace and non-violence, and erected several pillars throughout his empire to spread his edicts of morality and governance. The lion capital at Sarnath is one of the most famous of these pillars. It symbolizes not only the power of the empire, but also the promotion of ethical values such as compassion, harmony and justice.

In the modern national emblem of India, only three of the four lions are visible, as one is hidden at the back. Beneath the lions is a circular base adorned with engravings depicting important symbolic animals: an elephant, a horse, a bull and a lion, all moving in a circular motion. At the center of the base, the dharma chakra (wheel of law) is engraved, recalling the importance of justice and moral order. This chakra is also found at the center of the Indian flag, testifying to the profound influence of Ashoka's history on modern India.

Adopted as the national emblem in 1950, following India's independence, the Ashoka lion symbol embodies the continuity between India's glorious past and its modern aspirations. It reflects the ideals of sovereignty, peace and tolerance that post-independence India seeks to promote. It is a daily reminder that true power lies not in conquest, but in justice and the protection of humanitarian values, a lesson that Ashoka himself profoundly embodied.

Today, this symbol is omnipresent in the daily lives of Indians, serving as both a historical reminder and a moral inspiration. Whether engraved on coins or displayed on official documents, Ashoka's lion emblem continues to unite the nation under the principles of integrity and justice, timeless values that continue to guide modern India.

Fact 29 - Thali offers an explosion of Indian flavors

Thali is much more than a simple meal: it's a true gastronomic experience that represents the essence of Indian cuisine. Served on a circular platter, thali offers a variety of small dishes with contrasting flavors, from sweet to savory, from spicy to mild. Each region of India has its own version of thali, but it generally includes rice or bread (such as chapatis or puris), accompanied by vegetables, lentils (dal), chutneys and desserts, all carefully presented.

What makes thali unique is the diversity of textures and tastes that complement each other harmoniously. For example, a Rajasthani thali might include dishes based on millet or wheat, while a South Indian thali would feature rice, spicy curries, sambar and tangy pickles. Each bite is a discovery of the complex aromas that characterize Indian cuisine. It's a veritable journey through spices and culinary traditions that vary from region to region, but share a generosity and richness of flavors beyond compare.

Thali is also designed to be a balanced meal. Carefully chosen ingredients provide a combination of protein, carbohydrates, fiber and good fats. For example, dal, rich in vegetable protein, is often combined with fresh vegetables and rice or breads to provide energy. The spices used, such as turmeric, cumin and coriander, add not only taste but also health benefits, making thali both a delicious and nutritious meal.

The thali concept is not limited to food, it also reflects an Indian philosophy of life based on balance and harmony. Traditionally, the dishes of a thali are served at the same time, allowing guests to savor each element at their own pace, in an act of sharing and pleasure. This circular presentation also symbolizes the idea of unity in diversity, a central aspect of Indian culture where each dish has its own identity, yet contributes to a coherent whole.

Today, thali is not only a staple of Indian cuisine, but also an ambassador for Indian flavors around the world. Whether served in family restaurants or at major celebrations, this generous meal continues to captivate the taste buds and embody India's culinary richness. To eat a thali is to taste a piece of India's soul, combining tradition, diversity and pleasure on a single plate.

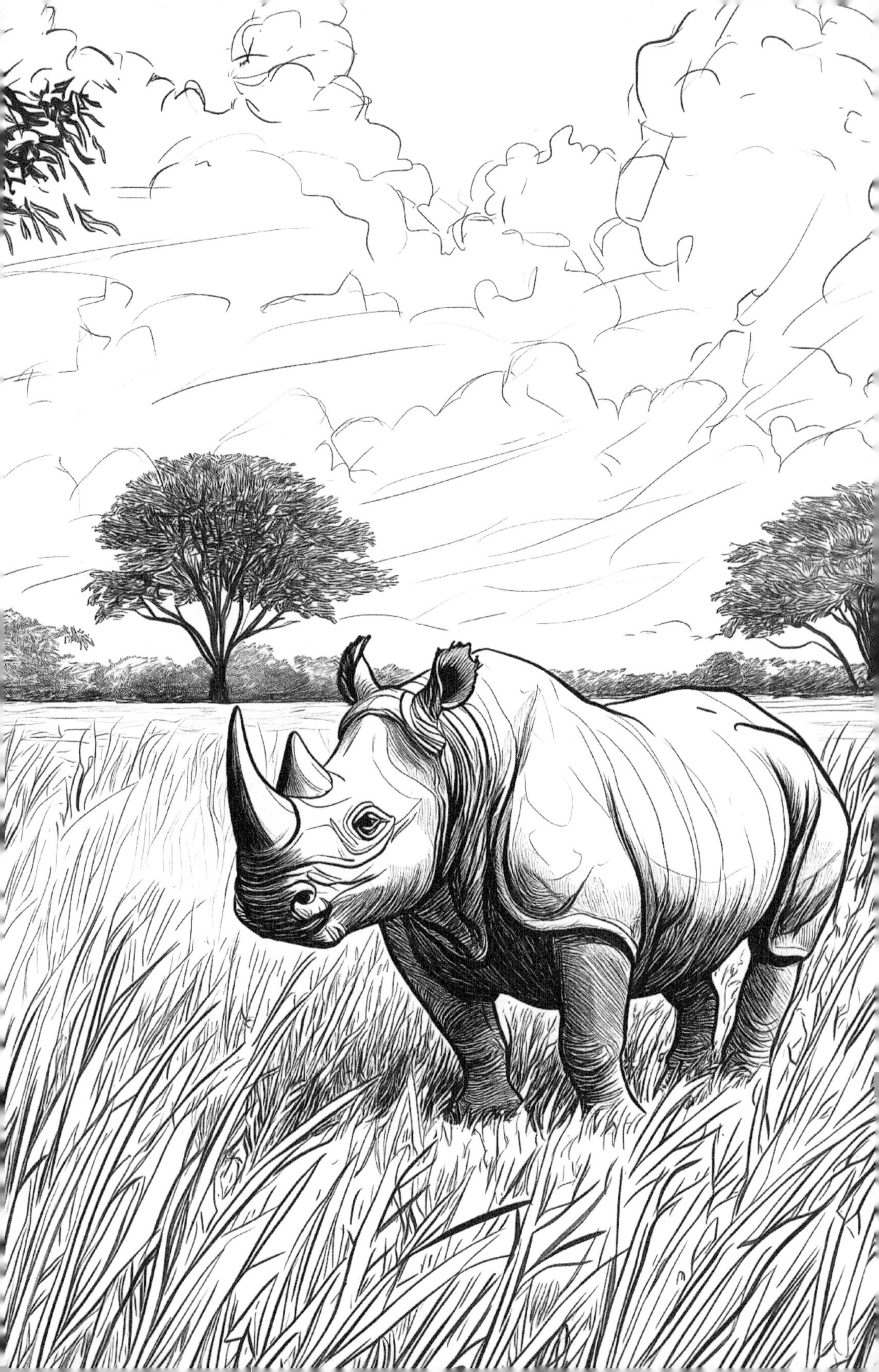

Fact 30 - Kaziranga National Park and its one-horned rhinos

Kaziranga National Park, located in the state of Assam, is one of India's most precious natural treasures. The park, a UNESCO World Heritage Site, is renowned for being home to the largest population of one-horned rhinos, also known as Indian rhinos. These majestic creatures, endowed with a single distinctive horn, are among India's most emblematic animal species, and their presence makes the park a crucial conservation area.

Kaziranga is a vast sanctuary covering more than 430 square kilometers, made up of grasslands, swamps and dense forests. The park is home to many other endangered species, including Asian elephants, Bengal tigers and wild buffalo. However, it is the one-horned rhinoceros that attracts international attention. The park is home to around 2,400 individuals, roughly two-thirds of the global population of this species. Thanks to its conservation efforts, Kaziranga has become a successful example of wildlife protection.

The conservation history of Kaziranga National Park is fascinating. In 1905, the protection of rhinos was initiated by Mary Curzon, wife of the British viceroy, Lord Curzon. After observing the alarming decline of this species, she urged her husband to establish a protected reserve. Today, the rigorous measures put in place, including the fight against poaching, have saved the one-horned rhinoceros from extinction, making Kaziranga a model for the management of fragile ecosystems.

As well as rhinos, Kaziranga is a paradise for nature lovers and biodiversity enthusiasts. The park is criss-crossed by numerous waterways, notably the Brahmaputra, and offers an ideal habitat for a diverse range of wildlife. Visitors can observe an incredible variety of migratory birds, reptiles and mammals in their natural environment. Safaris by jeep or elephant allow visitors to get up close and personal with rhinos in their wild habitat, an unforgettable experience.

Kaziranga National Park continues to play a vital role in preserving India's biodiversity. As the home of the one-horned rhinoceros, it serves as a reminder of the importance of global conservation efforts. This unique place, where wildlife thrives in an exceptional natural setting, is not only a source of pride for India, but also a symbol of commitment to the protection of endangered species and fragile ecosystems.

Fact 31 - India has 22 recognized official languages

India, with its impressive cultural diversity, is also one of the world's linguistically richest countries. It officially recognizes 22 languages in its Constitution, representing a wide variety of traditions, peoples and cultures. These languages, from diverse linguistic families, demonstrate India's unique plurality, where languages are not only means of communication, but also vectors of cultural and regional identity. Hindi is the most widely spoken language and one of the two official languages of the central government, the other being English.

India's 22 official languages include major languages such as Bengali, spoken mainly in West Bengal, Tamil, a classical language spoken in Tamil Nadu, and Telugu, predominant in the states of Andhra Pradesh and Telangana. Other important regional languages, such as Marathi, Gujarati and Punjabi, are spoken in specific regions, each reflecting the unique history and traditions of those areas. This makes India a veritable linguistic kaleidoscope, where several languages coexist on a daily basis.

Each language has a rich literary and cultural tradition. Tamil, for example, is one of the world's oldest languages still in use, with literature dating back over 2,000 years. Sanskrit, although not widely spoken today, is also an official language and remains crucial for religious and philosophical texts. These languages represent not only tools of communication, but also cultural heritages deeply rooted in India's history.

Language usage varies enormously from state to state. Each Indian state is free to choose its own official languages according to its majority population. In some states, such as Karnataka and Kerala, Kannada and Malayalam dominate respectively. Despite this diversity, English continues to serve as a common language between the states, particularly in the fields of commerce, education and politics, facilitating communication in a country where each region has its own linguistic heritage.

This incredible linguistic diversity makes India a unique model of cultural plurality. Far from being divisive, languages contribute to the unity of the country, giving each region its own identity, while at the same time forming an integral part of the Indian whole. The 22 recognized languages are just the tip of the iceberg, as India is home to hundreds of dialects, each with its own particularities and charm, forming a cultural mosaic as vast as it is fascinating.

Fact 32 - The Nilgiri is home to famous tea plantations

The Nilgiri Mountains in southern India are world-famous for their vast tea plantations. These hills, whose name means "blue mountains", form a spectacular landscape of green slopes covered with tea bushes as far as the eye can see. The cool, wet climate of the Nilgiri, with its regular rainfall and rich soils, makes it an ideal region for tea growing. These mountains are home to a tea renowned for its mild, slightly spicy flavor, which sets it apart from other Indian varieties such as Darjeeling or Assam.

Nilgiri tea is characterized by its lively, refreshing aroma. Grown at altitudes ranging from 1,000 to 2,500 meters, this tea grows all year round, unlike other regions where harvests are seasonal. It is particularly appreciated for its ability to blend with other flavors, making it a popular choice for iced teas and fragrant blends. Whether in whole leaf or in tea bags, Nilgiri tea is widely exported around the world, where it is appreciated for its unique taste and versatility.

The tea plantations of the Nilgiri have a long history, dating back to British colonial times, when tea was introduced to the region in the 19th century. Today, these plantations are a source of pride for India and play a major role in the local economy. Thousands of workers, often from families that have lived in the region for generations, harvest the young tea leaves by hand, a skill that requires great skill and care.

The Nilgiri region is also a popular tourist destination, thanks in no small part to its famous tea plantations. Towns such as Coonoor and Ooty are favorite haunts for visitors who come to discover the rolling hills, taste freshly brewed tea and learn more about the production process. These plantations offer guided tours, where you can follow every stage of tea processing, from leaf plucking to final packaging.

Beyond its worldwide renown, Nilgiri tea is deeply rooted in the daily lives of its inhabitants. It is omnipresent in local markets, homes and tea stalls, where people gather to chat over a steaming glass. Nilgiri tea is therefore not only a valuable export for India, but also an essential part of the culture and living heritage of this unique region.

Fact 33 - India is home to the world's largest democracy

India is often referred to as the world's largest democracy, due to its huge population of over 1.4 billion and its strong democratic system. Since independence in 1947, India has maintained its commitment to universal suffrage, allowing every citizen over the age of 18 to vote and participate in the democratic process. With over 900 million registered voters in the latest 2019 general elections, this is the largest democratic exercise ever held on the planet.

Elections in India, held every five years, mobilize a vast network of infrastructures. The country, which includes remote rural areas, mountains, deserts and dense megacities, faces enormous logistical challenges in ensuring that every voter can exercise his or her right to vote. Millions of civil servants are deployed across the country, and voting centers are set up in remote locations, sometimes even in areas where there is only one voter. This reflects India's commitment to ensuring that all its citizens, whatever their geographical circumstances, can participate in the democratic process.

India is a parliamentary democracy where representatives are elected at local, state and national level. The Lok Sabha, the lower house of the Indian Parliament, is made up of 543 members elected directly by citizens. These representatives play a crucial role in government formation, with the Prime Minister chosen from among them. This system ensures diverse representation, with voices from all over the country, whether rural or urban, from different ethnic or religious groups.

Since independence, India has maintained its democratic system despite political, social and economic challenges. The country's diversity, with its many languages, religions and cultures, is a source of both complexity and strength. Indian elections are a time when this diversity is fully expressed, allowing political parties representing a wide range of ideologies and interests to compete. The elections themselves are a celebration of popular participation, where political campaigning and debate are often vibrant and lively.

Today, India remains a model of democracy in the developing world. It has shown that even with such a vast and heterogeneous population, it is possible to maintain a functional and dynamic democratic system. Despite its many challenges, India continues to inspire other nations to embrace the ideals of freedom, equality and civic participation, proving that democracy can not only survive, but thrive under the most complex conditions.

Fact 34 - The Himalayas influence India's climate

The Himalayas, the world's highest mountain range, play a fundamental role in shaping India's climate. Stretching over 2,400 kilometers, this natural barrier separates the Indian subcontinent from the plateaus of Tibet and the rest of Central Asia. This imposing wall directly influences the monsoons, winds and temperatures that shape India's climate. Without the Himalayas, India's weather conditions would be radically different.

One of the Himalayas' major contributions is its ability to block cold winds from northern Central Asia. During the winter, these icy winds cannot cross the Himalayan barrier, enabling India to avoid the extremely low temperatures seen in regions at the same latitude. This keeps the plains of northern India relatively warm, even during the winter months. In the absence of the Himalayas, northern India could experience much harsher winters.

The Himalayas also influence the famous Indian monsoon. In summer, warm air from the northern plains attracts moist winds from the Indian Ocean. When these winds meet the Himalayan mountains, they are forced to rise, cooling the air and causing heavy rains. This phenomenon is crucial for Indian agriculture, which is largely dependent on monsoon rainfall. Without the Himalayas, this natural barrier, monsoon rains would be less intense and less predictable, making agriculture more difficult in many regions.

The role of the Himalayas is not limited to these meteorological phenomena. The mountain range's many glaciers are vital sources of water for India's great rivers, such as the Ganges, Yamuna and Brahmaputra. These rivers, fed by melting Himalayan glaciers, supply water to millions of people across India. By regulating the flow of water and maintaining river levels, the Himalayas guarantee water resources all year round, even during the dry season.

So the Himalayas are much more than just a mountain range. It acts as a natural shield and climate regulator, protecting and enriching life on the Indian subcontinent. By influencing the monsoon, blocking cold winds and nourishing rivers, the Himalayas play a vital role in India's environmental, economic and agricultural well-being.

Fact 35 - India launched a mission to Mars in 2013

In November 2013, India marked a major milestone in its space exploration with the successful launch of its first mission to Mars, called Mangalyaan or Mars Orbiter Mission (MOM). The launch, led by the Indian Space Research Organisation (ISRO), placed India among the few nations to have successfully sent a mission to the Red Planet. What makes this mission particularly remarkable is that it was successful on the first attempt, a feat that few countries have achieved, and at a relatively low cost compared with other similar missions.

The Mangalyaan mission had several scientific objectives, including the study of the Martian surface, atmosphere and composition. Equipped with sophisticated instruments, the probe notably studied the presence of methane, a gas that could indicate a form of life on Mars. The data collected by Mangalyaan have not only helped to enrich our understanding of the Red Planet, but have also positioned India as an emerging power in the space field.

One of the most impressive aspects of this mission was its cost: around 74 million dollars, far less than other similar missions around the world. This low budget, combined with the mission's technical success, demonstrated ISRO's ability to devise innovative and economically viable solutions for space exploration. In comparison, missions to Mars by other space agencies had much higher costs, making Mangalyaan a success story in low-cost space engineering.

Mangalyaan also had a strong symbolic impact for India. The success of this mission has strengthened national pride and put India on the world map as a burgeoning space power. The feat has inspired a new generation of scientists, engineers and students in India, who see space exploration as a field in which their country can excel. It is also a signal that India has the capacity to compete with the great nations in cutting-edge fields such as space technology.

With this mission to Mars, India has demonstrated its capacity for advanced space exploration. Mangalyaan remains a milestone not only for ISRO, but also for the entire country, proving that even with limited resources, India can achieve exceptional feats and actively participate in the discovery of the mysteries of our universe.

Fact 36 - The compass used for the first time in India

India was one of the first places where the compass was used for navigation, and it played a crucial role in the development of maritime and land exploration. Called the "Matsya Yantra" in ancient texts, the Indian compass was used by sailors and merchants to orient themselves at sea, long before this instrument was used in Europe. The device was simple but effective: it used a magnetized needle floating or suspended in the water to indicate north, thus facilitating navigation.

In Indian history, maritime navigation has always been essential for trade and exchange with other civilizations. Maritime trade routes linking India to Southeast Asia, China and the Middle East were very active, and the compass played a key role in these exchanges. Indian navigators used them to travel across the Indian Ocean, a region where monsoon winds often complicated navigation. The compass helped to correct direction according to these changing winds.

The Indian compass was not just a maritime tool. It was also used by explorers and traders for overland travel. It helped them traverse the vast plains and mountain ranges of the Indian subcontinent. Thanks to this instrument, trade caravans crossing northern India, the deserts of Rajasthan or the dense forests of the south could find their way and reach their destinations, even in difficult conditions.

Indian knowledge of astronomy and geography played a major role in the invention and use of the compass. Ancient Indian scholars were fascinated by the observation of stars and celestial phenomena. They understood the importance of orientation for commercial and military expeditions. Ancient writings, such as those of the philosopher Varahamihira, mention navigational instruments using terrestrial magnetism, proof that India was a pioneer in this field.

Today, the invention and early use of the compass in India is considered a milestone in the history of science and navigation. This tool revolutionized the way people traveled and interacted, paving the way for wider explorations and more extensive trade networks. India's contribution to technological innovation is reflected in this simple but essential instrument, which changed the course of civilizational history.

Fact 37 - The Brihadeswara temple is made entirely of granite

The Brihadeswara temple, located in Thanjavur in the state of Tamil Nadu, is one of the greatest architectural wonders of ancient India. Built in the early 11th century during the reign of Emperor Raja Raja Chola I, the temple is constructed entirely of granite. This material, known for its strength and durability, was used to erect this colossal monument, which continues to amaze visitors with its imposing size and sculptural finesse. This choice of granite is all the more impressive given that it is not available in the vicinity of the site, raising questions about the techniques and means of transport used at the time.

The temple is dedicated to the god Shiva, and its vimana (main tower) rises to a height of over 60 meters, making it one of the tallest temple structures in India. At the top of the tower is a massive granite block weighing around 80 tonnes. How this stone was hoisted to such a height remains a mystery, but some theories suggest the use of giant ramps or sophisticated lifting systems. This masterpiece of engineering demonstrates the exceptional technical mastery of the Cholas, a dynasty famous for its advances in architecture and art.

Each stone of the Brihadeswara temple is adorned with detailed carvings, depicting mythological scenes, divine figures and intricate representations of religious rituals and dances. These carvings, carved in granite, testify to the skill of the craftsmen of the time. Among the most remarkable works of art are representations of the tandava, Shiva's cosmic dance, which express both divine energy and artistic beauty. The precision of the details carved into this hard rock is a demonstration of the finesse and skill of the stone carvers.

The Brihadeswara temple is not only a place of worship, but also a symbol of the power and grandeur of the Chola empire. The building testifies to the importance the rulers placed on religion and art, and their desire to leave a lasting legacy. To this day, the temple is still in use, attracting pilgrims from all over the world who come to admire this exceptional monument to Shiva, but also to marvel at the ingenuity and vision of its builders.

A UNESCO World Heritage Site, Brihadeswara Temple remains a dazzling example of Dravidian architecture and a testament to the creativity and ambition of the Chola kings. Its immense structure, built entirely of granite, defies the centuries and continues to tell the fascinating story of a time when ancient India shone with artistic, religious and scientific advances.

Fact 38 - The Lotus Temple looks like a huge flower

The Lotus Temple, located in New Delhi, is one of the most remarkable and distinctive buildings in modern India. Built in the shape of a lotus, a sacred flower in many Indian traditions, the temple impresses with its unique, elegant architecture. Inaugurated in 1986, it is one of the most visited temples in the world, attracting millions of visitors every year, whether they come to pray or simply to admire its design. Designed by Iranian architect Fariborz Sahba, the Lotus Temple is a place of worship for the Baha'i faith, which advocates the unity of humanity and all religions.

The building is formed of 27 white marble petals, arranged in three rows that open progressively towards the sky, imitating the shape of a lotus flower in full bloom. This design symbolizes purity, peace and spirituality, essential concepts in the Baha'i Faith. Each petal is meticulously carved and constructed from white marble imported from Greece, the same material used to build the famous Taj Mahal. The structure, though bold and contemporary, blends harmoniously into its surroundings, inspiring a sense of serenity and awe.

The temple is surrounded by nine water basins, which accentuate the impression of a flower floating on a lake. These basins play not only an aesthetic role, but also a practical one: they help to naturally cool the interior of the temple, a shining example of ecological architecture. As a space of worship open to all, Lotus Temple is a place where no religious images are present, and where anyone, whatever their faith, can meditate or pray in silence. It is a space of spiritual peace, accessible to all, regardless of creed.

The Lotus Temple's design also reflects the principles of the Baha'i Faith, which advocates the unity of humanity and equality between religions. There are no specific sermons or rituals. The sacred texts of all major religions can be read or recited inside, and the building is deliberately devoid of any visible religious decoration, reinforcing the message of inclusivity and universality. This commitment to unity is what distinguishes the temple from other places of worship, and makes it unique in its approach.

The Lotus Temple is not only a spiritual symbol, but also a feat of engineering and modern architecture. Its bold, visionary design makes it a landmark for India and the world. By blending traditional and contemporary aesthetic elements, it embodies both India's spiritual heritage and its aspiration for global unity.

Fact 39 - The decimal system was invented in India

The decimal system, which we use every day for counting and calculations, was invented in India over 2,000 years ago. This system, based on base 10, has revolutionized the way numbers are processed throughout the world. One of the major contributions of this system is the introduction of the digit zero, which makes it possible to create new combinations of digits and express numbers with greater precision. The Indian mathematician Aryabhata and other scholars played a key role in formalizing this system, which was subsequently adopted worldwide.

Before the invention of the decimal system, many peoples used much more complex and impractical counting methods. The Indian system, simple and efficient, was soon recognized for its ease of use. It simplified calculations, made mathematics teaching more accessible and facilitated commercial transactions. Thanks to the clarity of this system, numbers could be extended infinitely simply by adding zeros or powers of 10.

The role of the zero in the decimal system cannot be underestimated. It was this invention that gave birth to modern mathematics, as the zero allows digits to be positioned and multiplied or divided with ease. This concept, so simple today, was a real revolution at the time. The term "zero" itself comes from the Sanskrit word "śūnya", meaning "void". This idea of representing emptiness with a single symbol transformed the way mathematicians thought about numbers and their interactions.

The influence of this system spread beyond India. Through the Arabs, who passed on this knowledge to Europeans in the Middle Ages, the decimal system spread throughout the world. The numbers we use today, known as Arabic numerals, actually originated in India. They have become the global standard, replacing older systems such as Roman numerals, which were much less practical for complex calculations.

Today, the decimal system is used in almost every field, from finance to science and technology. It has paved the way for major advances in mathematics and enabled innovations in disciplines such as physics, astronomy and economics. The fact that this system originated in India testifies to the immense contribution made by Indian civilization to the development of scientific and mathematical thought, influencing our everyday lives to this day.

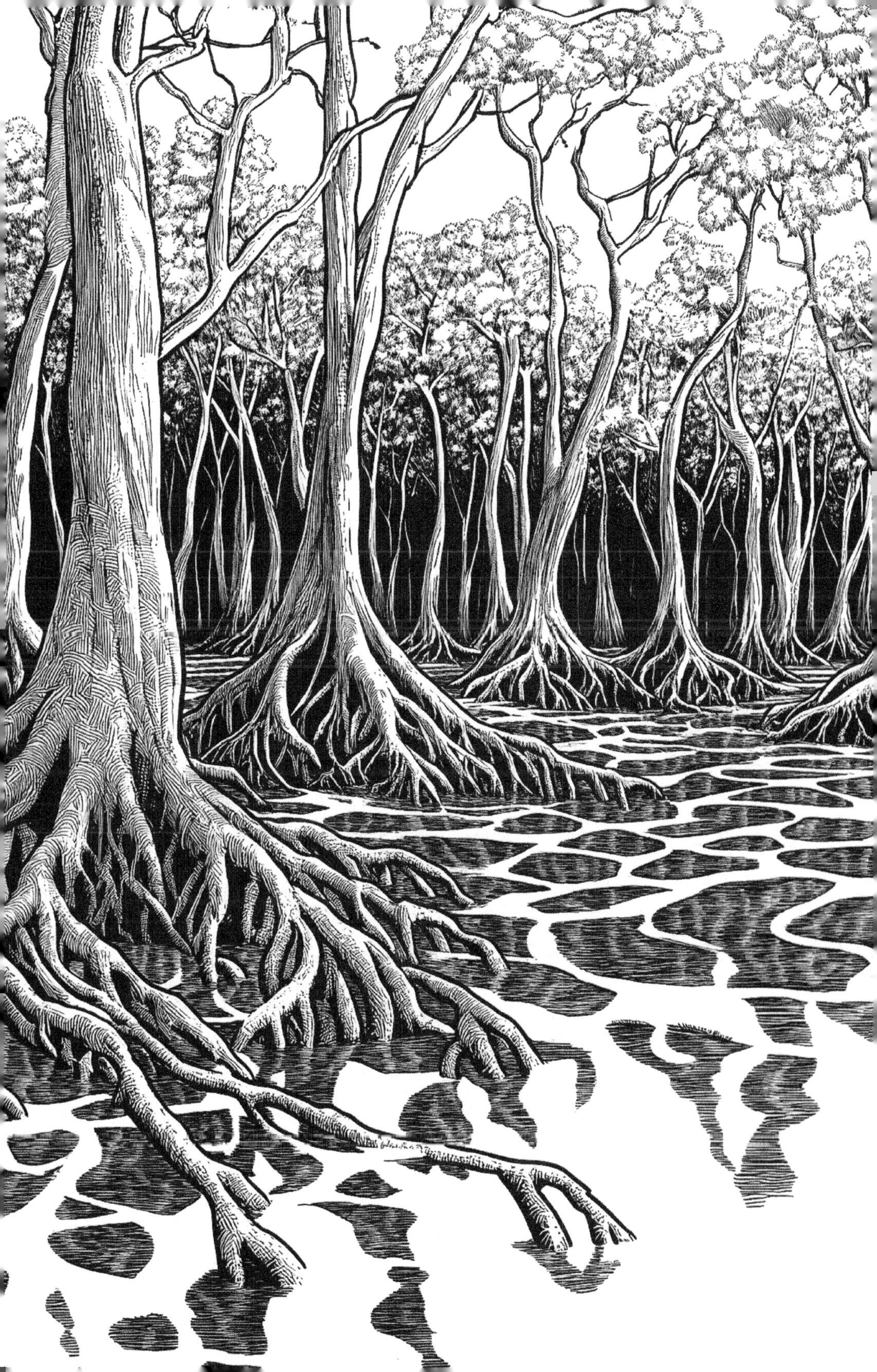

Fact 40 - Sundarbans mangroves naturally filter water

The Sundarbans, stretching between India and Bangladesh, form the world's largest mangrove forest. Not only is this unique region home to exceptional biodiversity, it also plays a crucial role in water purification. Mangroves act as a natural filter, removing impurities from sea and river water. The complex roots of these trees slow the flow of water, allowing sediments, pollutants and toxins to settle out before the water flows back into the surrounding ecosystems. This process improves water quality, while preserving the health of coastal ecosystems.

The aerial roots of mangroves, known as pneumatophores, are particularly effective at filtration. By capturing suspended particles, they reduce the amount of pollutants in the water, protecting the marine and terrestrial creatures that depend on them. Fish, crustaceans and other aquatic organisms living in the Sundarbans benefit directly from this natural filtration system. What's more, by slowing the flow of water, mangroves limit soil erosion and reinforce coastal stability.

In addition to their role as filters, the mangroves of the Sundarbans play an essential role in protecting coastal areas from storms and tides. Their dense network of roots forms a natural barrier that absorbs part of the wave energy, reducing the impact of floods and cyclones. This ability to act as a buffer zone between sea and land limits the damage caused by natural disasters, a valuable asset for local populations living in these vulnerable regions.

The Sundarbans are also an important source of blue carbon, a term used to describe the carbon stored in coastal ecosystems such as mangroves, marshes and seagrass beds. This carbon storage contributes to the fight against climate change by capturing and retaining carbon dioxide from the atmosphere. Sundarbans mangroves therefore play a key role not only in protecting local ecosystems, but also in global climate regulation.

Today, protecting the Sundarbans is vital to maintaining these vital ecosystem services. In addition to filtering water, mangroves support biodiversity, protect coastlines and help combat climate change. This UNESCO World Heritage site is a perfect illustration of the importance of natural ecosystems in environmental balance, providing a powerful example of the interconnection between nature and human communities.

Fact 41 - Chess was invented in India

Chess, as we know it today, has its origins in India, where it was invented under the name of Chaturanga in the 6th century. This strategic game, whose name means "four divisions of the army" in Sanskrit, represented the main military units of the time: chariots, elephants, cavalry and infantry. These four army pieces were transformed over time to become the rooks, knights, bishops and pawns of modern chess. This game, based on tactics and strategy, quickly became popular throughout Asia, before spreading to Persia, Europe and the rest of the world.

Chaturanga was played by four players, each controlling an army. The aim of the game was to use one's pieces strategically to capture the opponent's pieces, a concept that has remained fundamental to the modern version of chess. The game differed from other board games of the time in its emphasis on reflection and foresight. Unlike games based solely on luck, such as dice, Chaturanga required players to think ahead about their moves and anticipate their opponents' actions.

As the game spread, it evolved into what we know today as chess. In Persia, it took the name of Shatranj, a game played with two players, where the rules began to resemble those of today's chess. When chess reached Europe in the Middle Ages, the pieces took on more familiar forms. For example, elephants became fools, and the royal advisor became the queen. The game's intellectual dimension made it popular among European nobility, who saw it as a metaphor for the political and military struggles of the time.

Chess continued to evolve in the West, with the addition of new rules that accelerated the pace of play, notably the greater freedom of movement granted to the queen and bishops. However, despite these changes, chess has retained its original spirit, that of a game where strategic thinking and the ability to anticipate are paramount. Today, chess is played all over the world, from the street to the biggest international competitions, but its origins remain deeply rooted in Indian culture.

The link between India and chess is still very strong. Many international chess champions, such as Viswanathan Anand, hail from India, and the country continues to be an important center for the promotion of the game. The history of chess is thus a testament to India's cultural and intellectual heritage, which has given the world a game that is both timeless and universal, played by millions of people in both playful and competitive contexts.

Fact 42 - Extreme temperatures in the Thar Desert

The Thar Desert, located mainly in the Indian state of Rajasthan, is one of the world's largest arid deserts. This desert, also known as the Great Indian Desert, is famous for its extreme temperatures. In summer, temperatures can soar to 50°C, while in winter, they sometimes drop below zero at night. This brutal variation between day and night, as well as hot and cold seasons, makes the Thar unique in terms of climate, but also in terms of the challenges faced by the people who live there.

The intense heat of the Thar Desert is caused by several factors. Firstly, the absence of vegetation and water over vast expanses prevents humidity from being maintained, amplifying the effects of the sun. Hot winds blowing from the west exacerbate this heat, making the Thar a region where summer survival relies on well-established strategies, such as thick-walled houses to insulate against the heat, or the use of loose, lightweight clothing to protect the skin.

In contrast, nights in the Thar Desert can be surprisingly cold, especially in winter. This is due to the sand's inability to retain the heat accumulated during the day. As a result, temperatures drop rapidly when the sun goes down, creating an environment where thermal amplitudes are considerable. It is this ability of the desert to go from one extreme to another that makes it fascinating, both climatically and ecologically.

Despite these difficult conditions, the Thar is home to a rich and surprising biodiversity. Animals such as the camel, perfectly adapted to this climate, are essential to the daily life of the local population. Xerophytic plants, capable of storing water and resisting drought, also thrive in this arid environment. Human ingenuity and nature's ability to adapt to extreme conditions are revealed in this landscape, where life has found ways to flourish despite the climatic challenges.

The Thar is not only a desert of extreme temperatures, it's also a culturally rich region. The inhabitants, mainly Rajasthani, have developed lifestyles adapted to this harsh environment over the centuries. The festivals, crafts and colorful traditions of this region bear witness to the resilience and creativity of the local people. This desert, often perceived as a hostile environment, is also a place where human culture and nature coexist in harmony.

Fact 43 - Mount Abu, an oasis in the middle of the desert

Mount Abu, perched at an altitude of 1,220 metres, is a veritable oasis in the heart of the Thar Desert, in the state of Rajasthan. It is the only mountain resort in this arid region, offering a striking contrast to the surrounding desert expanses. Surrounded by lush forests, crystal-clear lakes and refreshing waterfalls, this verdant massif attracts tourists and pilgrims alike, seeking solace and spirituality. Its cool, green landscapes make it an ideal escape from the extreme temperatures of the desert.

One of Mount Abu's highlights is Lake Nakki, a naturally occurring body of water surrounded by lush green hills. According to legend, this lake was dug by gods with their fingernails to protect the city. The site is not only a place of recreation for visitors, but is also rich in spirituality and local myths. Boat trips allow you to enjoy the beauty of the surrounding landscape while discovering what some call the "sacred lake".

Mount Abu is also famous for its Dilwara Jain temples, dating from the 11th and 13th centuries. Built entirely of white marble, these temples are renowned for the finesse of their carvings. Every column, ceiling and wall is meticulously engraved with floral motifs, divine figures and scenes from the lives of the tirthankaras (spiritual masters of Jainism). The main temple, dedicated to Adinath, attracts pilgrims from all over India, as well as visitors fascinated by the grandeur and perfection of the architecture.

Mount Abu's temperate climate makes it a popular destination, especially in summer when temperatures reach extremes in the plains of Rajasthan. Its forests are home to a rich variety of wildlife, including leopards, monkeys and several species of exotic birds. Mount Abu also offers spectacular panoramic views, particularly from Guru Shikhar, the mountain's highest point, where visitors can admire awe-inspiring vistas of the desert and beyond.

Mount Abu is much more than just a place of refuge from the desert heat. It's a place of unspoilt nature, spirituality and culture. Its soothing atmosphere and enchanting landscapes make it a special oasis, where history, religion and nature meet in perfect harmony.

Fact 44 - The king cobra detects movement with its tongue

The king cobra, one of India's most fearsome snakes, has an astonishing ability to detect movement: it uses its bifid tongue. Unlike most animals, this snake doesn't rely solely on sight or hearing. In fact, its highly sensitive tongue enables it to capture chemical particles in the air, which it then sends to its Jacobson's organ, located in its mouth. This organ analyzes the information and helps the cobra locate its prey or spot possible dangers.

When the king cobra sticks out its tongue, it picks up the microscopic odors and vibrations left in the air by other animals. This ability is particularly useful in dark environments, where visibility is poor. Using this technique, the cobra can track prey even in low-light conditions. It can sense the movements of a small mammal or another snake from several meters away, giving it a great advantage when hunting.

The king cobra is the world's longest venomous snake, sometimes reaching over five meters in length. It lives mainly in the tropical forests and grasslands of the Indian subcontinent. Its venom is extremely powerful, capable of killing an elephant in a matter of hours. However, this impressive snake generally prefers to avoid interaction with humans. It only attacks if it feels threatened, using its ability to detect movement to assess the situation and flee if necessary.

The hunting behavior of the king cobra is fascinating. Rather than pouncing on its prey, it is patient and uses its senses to track and discreetly approach its target. In addition to its tongue, the snake is able to detect vibrations on the ground thanks to its long, slender body. Every movement of its prey is registered with precision, enabling it to attack at just the right moment. This combination of hyper-developed senses makes the king cobra a formidable predator.

In India, the king cobra is revered in certain regions and plays an important role in local myths and culture. Despite its dangerous nature, it is often considered a symbol of protection and power. Thanks to its unique abilities, such as the use of its tongue to detect movement, the king cobra continues to amaze as well as impress those who come across it.

Fact 45 - India produces the largest quantity of curry in the world

India is known the world over for its curries, dishes rich in flavor and spice. The term "curry" refers to a wide variety of sauce-based dishes, often prepared with a blend of spices. India not only produces the largest quantity of curry in the world, it is also the largest producer of the spices essential to its preparation, such as turmeric, cumin, coriander and cardamom. These spices, grown in abundance in regions such as Kerala and Gujarat, are at the heart of Indian cuisine.

Indian curry is far from being a simple, uniform sauce. Each region of the country has its own variations on curries, influenced by local culture, climate and availability of ingredients. For example, in southern India, curries tend to be spicier and often coconut-based, while in the north, dairy products such as yoghurt or ghee are more frequently used to sweeten dishes. This diversity makes curry a central and symbolic element of India's enormous culinary wealth.

What particularly distinguishes Indian curry from other dishes around the world is the use of spice blends, often called masalas. These blends vary from dish to dish and region to region, but they are all carefully measured to create a unique balance of flavors: spicy, sweet, bitter, sour. The famous garam masala, for example, is a blend of spices used to enhance many curries, bringing a depth of flavor that is difficult to imitate. It's this art of blending spices that makes Indian curries so famous.

As well as being a national dish, Indian curry has also conquered the world. From Asia to Europe, via North America, there are countless adaptations of curry, influenced by Indian migration or the spice trade. However, the curries prepared in Indian homes, often using recipes handed down from generation to generation, remain the most authentic, preserving the very soul of this ancestral cuisine.

By producing large quantities of curry, India maintains a vibrant culinary tradition that reflects not only its cultural diversity, but also its connection with the land and its natural resources. From local markets to major exports, India continues to share this spicy richness with the rest of the world, cultivating it in its fields, homes and restaurants.

Fact 46 - The Siachen glacier is the highest in the world

The Siachen glacier, located in the Karakoram region of northern India, is the world's highest glacier. Perched at an average altitude of 5,400 meters, it stretches for some 76 kilometers, making it one of the longest glaciers outside the polar regions. This glacier, often referred to as the "third pole", plays a key role in the geography of the Himalayas and attracts attention for its extreme conditions and strategic importance.

This glacier is located in an area where temperatures can drop to -50°C in winter. These extreme weather conditions make life and survival difficult in this region. The freezing cold and lack of oxygen at such an altitude make the Siachen glacier an inhospitable place for humans, but despite this, it remains a strategically important point for India, not least because of its geographical position close to the border with Pakistan and China.

In addition to its geopolitical importance, the Siachen glacier is an extremely valuable freshwater reserve for India. As the source of several rivers that feed the region, the glacier plays an essential role in the water supply of millions of people living in the plains of northern India. With global warming, Himalayan glaciers are melting at a faster rate, and studies show that this could have a major impact on water resources throughout the region.

The Siachen glacier is also a site of interest to scientists. Its extreme altitude and harsh conditions make it a unique natural laboratory for studying climate change, the ecology of glacial zones and the effects of extreme cold on living organisms. Researchers regularly visit this region to monitor the evolution of the ice cap and to better understand the long-term impacts of global warming on Himalayan glaciers.

Today, the Siachen glacier symbolizes not only the beauty and power of nature, but also the challenges faced by mankind in preserving these unique environments. One of the world's most isolated and inaccessible places, it continues to fascinate with its grandeur and its ecological and geopolitical importance.

Fact 47 - India has the world's largest population of sacred cows

In India, cows occupy a special place, both religiously and culturally. India is home to the world's largest population of sacred cows, numbering some 300 million, many of which are venerated as part of the Hindu religion. The cow, symbol of fertility, gentleness and non-violence, is associated with the goddess Lakshmi, figure of prosperity and wealth. This sacred status protects them from mistreatment, and they are free to roam the streets, often fed and respected by the locals.

The importance of the cow in Indian culture goes back millennia, when it is mentioned in Vedic texts as a sacred animal. It is seen as a gift from nature, providing milk, clarified butter (ghee), and manure, used as fertilizer and fuel. The cow is thus considered an essential member of Indian society, contributing to daily life and agriculture, while being respected for its benevolent and generous nature.

Ghee, for example, made from cow's milk, is used in many religious rituals, in traditional cooking and even in Ayurvedic medicine. This product perfectly illustrates the sacred link between cows and Hindu spirituality. Cows are not just a source of food, but a living symbol of life, nourishing the bodies and souls of Indians for generations.

In some parts of India, specific festivals are held in honor of cows, such as Gopashtami, a festival during which cows are bathed, decorated and worshipped. This special day marks the importance of cows in society, beyond their simple function as domestic animals. Cows are blessed, and families pray for their protection and for their herds to prosper.

Today, the status of cows in India continues to be protected by laws in many states, which prohibit their slaughter. This respect for sacred cows is evident in all aspects of Indian life, where they symbolize the interconnection between man and nature, spirituality and everyday life. The cow, in all its simplicity and utility, embodies a figure both humble and divine, deeply rooted in India's cultural identity.

Fact 48 - The Kailasa temple is carved entirely out of rock

The Kailasa temple, located in Ellora in the state of Maharashtra, is an architectural masterpiece carved entirely from rock. This monumental temple dedicated to Shiva is part of a vast complex of 34 caves, but it stands out for its impressive size and the technical feat it represents. Built in the 8th century under the Rashtrakuta dynasty, the Kailasa temple is unique in that it was not built piece by piece, but carved directly into a single basalt cliff.

What makes the Kailasa temple so extraordinary is the fact that the craftsmen started carving at the top of the rock, then gradually worked their way down. They removed around 200,000 tons of rock to shape this temple, which is an incredible amount considering the limited tools available at the time. The temple covers an area of 2,000 square metres and stands over 30 metres high. Every detail, from the columns to the sculptures of the deities, has been meticulously fashioned from the rock, giving the impression that the temple has sprung from the mountain itself.

The temple's architecture is inspired by Mount Kailash, the sacred mountain in Hinduism, believed to be the home of Shiva. Inside, the main sanctuary houses a lingam, the symbol of Shiva, and is surrounded by detailed sculptures representing various Hindu deities. Every corner of the temple is adorned with mythological figures, majestic animals such as elephants, and epic scenes from India's great sacred texts, such as the Ramayana and the Mahabharata.

The Kailasa temple is not only an architectural feat; it is also a symbol of spiritual devotion. It is said that King Krishna I of the Rashtrakutas ordered its construction to demonstrate his piety and devotion to Shiva. He even promised his queen to build such a majestic temple in record time, defying the laws of traditional architecture. Although it took several years to complete, the temple remains a testament to the ingenuity and skill of ancient Indian sculptors.

Today, the Kailasa temple attracts visitors and pilgrims from all over the world. A UNESCO World Heritage Site, it is a living testimony to the excellence of ancient Indian art and the depth of Hindu spirituality. The temple continues to captivate with its mystery, beauty and technical prowess, offering a fascinating insight into the history and culture of ancient India.

Fact 49 - Chapatis are Indian yeast-free wafers

Chapatis, also known as roti in some regions, are yeast-free wafers that play a central role in Indian cuisine. Made mainly from whole-wheat flour, chapatis are both simple and nutritious. They are prepared by mixing flour with water to form a dough, which is then flattened into thin patties before being cooked on a pan called a tava. This process, though seemingly modest, makes chapatis an essential part of traditional Indian meals.

Chapatis are popular throughout India, but regional variations may differ. In the north of the country, they are often eaten on a daily basis, accompanying vegetable curries, lentils or meats. They serve as a base for absorbing the rich sauces and flavors of the dishes that accompany them. Their supple texture and neutral taste make them a perfect complement to a wide range of dishes. What's more, unlike other breads, chapatis are entirely yeast-free, giving them a finer, denser texture.

The process of baking chapatis is also a demonstration of culinary skill. After being rolled out, the dough is placed on the tava, where it begins to cook slowly. As it does so, the heat swells the cake, creating little pockets of air that make the chapati soft. Some families then use a direct flame to further puff up the cake, giving it a light, airy texture and a slight smoky flavor.

Chapatis also have great cultural significance in India. In many regions, the preparation of these wafers is a daily ritual, handed down from generation to generation. Family meals, especially in rural areas, often begin with the preparation of chapatis, a moment of sharing between members of the household. This simple but essential bread symbolizes the warmth of hospitality and the importance of home-cooked meals in Indian culture.

What's more, chapatis are a versatile food. Not only can they accompany savory dishes, but they are sometimes used to wrap vegetables or pieces of meat, creating a kind of traditional sandwich. In some regions, they are also served with ghee (clarified butter) or sugar to make them even tastier. Whether used as a staple or as an ingredient in more complex recipes, chapatis remain a staple of Indian cuisine, appreciated for their simplicity and versatility.

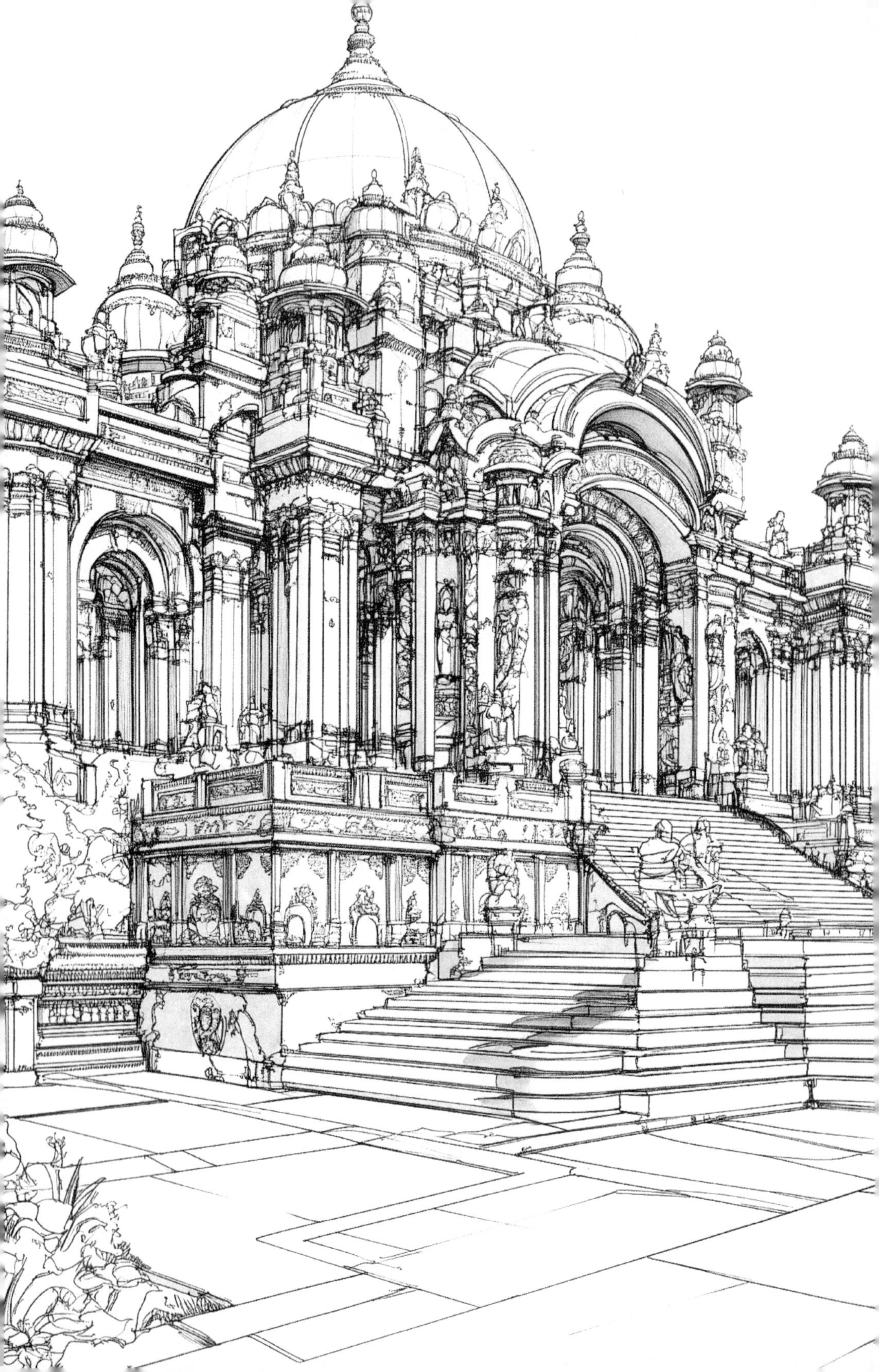

Fact 50 - The Akshardham temple is the largest in the world

The Akshardham Temple in Delhi is recognized as the world's largest Hindu temple. Inaugurated in 2005, this impressive monument is an architectural marvel dedicated to Bhagwan Swaminarayan, a revered Hindu figure. The complex extends over more than 40 hectares, with the main building measuring 43 metres high, 96 metres wide and 110 metres long. Its construction mobilized some 11,000 craftsmen and volunteers, who used pink sandstone and white marble to build this breathtaking structure.

The Akshardham Temple is much more than a place of worship. It is designed to illustrate Indian spiritual values, culture and traditions. Every corner of the temple is decorated with intricately carved sculptures depicting deities, animals and scenes from Hindu mythology. The central mandir houses a solid gold statue of Swaminarayan and is surrounded by several shrines dedicated to other Hindu deities such as Vishnu, Shiva and Parvati. The richness of detail and finesse of the sculptures make this a monumental work of art.

In addition to the mandir, the complex offers interactive exhibitions and performances that trace the history, philosophy and values of Hinduism. Attractions include an IMAX cinema showing a film on the life of Swaminarayan and a cultural cruise that takes visitors through 10,000 years of Indian history. Another fascinating feature is the Yagnapurush Kund, the world's largest step fountain, featuring light and water shows telling mythological stories.

The Akshardham temple was built without the use of concrete or steel, using traditional Hindu temple construction techniques. Each stone was assembled with precision, demonstrating ancient craftsmanship that reflects the builders' attachment to spiritual values. The temple also incorporates modern ecological concepts, with water treatment systems and environmentally-friendly practices.

Today, Akshardham is not just a temple, but a living symbol of Indian culture, spirituality and architecture. It attracts millions of visitors from all over the world every year, curious to admire its unique architecture and learn more about India's history and traditions.

Fact 51 - Cotton grown for the first time in India

India is the cradle of cotton cultivation, one of the most widely used fibers in the world today. Over 5,000 years ago, during the Indus Valley civilization, ancient Indians grew and used cotton to make clothing. Archaeological digs in cities such as Mohenjo-Daro have revealed traces of cotton fabrics, proving that Indians had already mastered the art of weaving long before the practice spread elsewhere in the world.

The hot, dry climate of regions like Gujarat and Maharashtra was ideal for growing cotton. Thanks to this abundance, India soon became a world center for the production and export of cotton fabrics, known as calico. These light, colorful fabrics traveled to distant lands such as Egypt, Greece and Rome, creating a flourishing trade that contributed to the prosperity of Indian civilizations.

The cotton-making process, although manual in those days, was sophisticated. The Indians had mastered the art of spinning, which involved transforming cotton fibers into threads, then weaving them into fine, durable textiles. They were also renowned for their ability to dye these fabrics using natural pigments, giving rise to vibrant textiles sought after the world over.

In addition to its commercial use, cotton played an essential role in the daily lives of the Indians. It was used to make clothes suited to hot, humid climates, but also for domestic purposes such as bedding. Cotton's popularity spread to all levels of Indian society, and it has remained a symbol of elegance and comfort over the centuries.

Even today, India remains one of the world's largest cotton producers. This fiber, once cultivated by the ancient Indus civilizations, continues to play a crucial role in the country's economy and culture. More than just a raw material, cotton represents a profound historical and cultural heritage, linking India's glorious past to its present.

Fact 52 - The Golden Temple of Amritsar is covered in real gold

The Golden Temple of Amritsar, or Harmandir Sahib, is one of the holiest sites in Sikhism. Located in northern India, in the city of Amritsar, this iconic temple is world-famous for its dome covered in real gold, giving it an unrivalled splendour. Built in the 16th century by the fifth Sikh Guru, Guru Arjan, it was conceived as a place of worship open to all, regardless of religion, status or gender.

The temple's dome is covered with 750 kg of gold, an addition made in the 19th century by Maharaja Ranjit Singh, a powerful Sikh ruler. This finely-worked gold shimmers in the sunlight and is beautifully reflected in the sacred pool surrounding the temple, called Amrit Sarovar. This body of water is considered sacred by the Sikhs, who believe in its purifying properties. The reflection of the temple in these waters adds to the impression of majesty and serenity that emanates from the site.

The temple's architecture is a harmonious blend of Hindu and Islamic elements, symbolizing Sikhism's openness to all cultures. The meticulously carved details on the walls and arches, as well as the marble carvings, bear witness to remarkable craftsmanship. Inside, the temple houses the Guru Granth Sahib, the sacred text of Sikhism, which is recited continuously throughout the day.

The Golden Temple is also famous for its langar, a community kitchen that serves free meals to thousands of visitors every day, regardless of caste, creed or social status. This service, based on the Sikh philosophy of seva (selfless service), is one of the largest langars in the world. It is a powerful example of the generosity and equality advocated by Sikhism.

Every year, millions of people visit the Golden Temple, Sikhs and non-Sikhs alike. Beyond its glittering gold, this place is a symbol of peace, devotion and selfless service. The Golden Temple continues to be a center of spirituality that inspires admiration and devotion, not only for its architectural beauty, but also for the values it embodies.

Fact 53 - The red panda protected in the state of Sikkim

The red panda, a rare and mysterious creature, finds refuge in the forests of Sikkim, a mountainous state in northeast India. This endangered species is protected by local and international initiatives to preserve its natural habitat. Unlike its giant Chinese cousin, the red panda is much smaller and spends most of its time in the trees, feeding on bamboo, fruit and insects.

The Khangchendzonga National Park in Sikkim is one of the sanctuaries where the red panda can be observed in its natural environment. With its dense forest cover and high altitude, this ecosystem is ideal for this mammal, which prefers temperate and humid forests. The park, a UNESCO World Heritage Site, is home to several dozen red pandas and is at the heart of conservation efforts in India.

Efforts to protect the red panda are not limited to preserving its habitat. Awareness-raising projects are also carried out with local communities to reduce poaching and forest destruction. Indian authorities are working with international organizations such as the Red Panda Network to monitor red panda populations and combat threats to the species, including deforestation and poaching.

The red panda, with its glossy red coat and bushy tail, has become a symbol of conservation in northeast India. It is also the official mascot of the state of Sikkim, where it is respected for its rarity and beauty. This small arboreal animal plays a key role in the region's ecological balance, contributing to seed dispersal and forest health.

Today, thanks to these joint conservation efforts, the Sikkim red panda is better protected than it was in the past. However, the threat of extinction remains real, and it is crucial that initiatives continue to ensure that future generations can continue to admire this unique little mammal in the forests of Sikkim.

Fact 54 - India is home to the world's largest wild elephant sanctuary

India's largest wild elephant sanctuary is the Periyar Elephant Reserve in the state of Kerala. This vast reserve, covering over 900 km², is dedicated to the protection of these majestic pachyderms. The elephants live in total freedom in a natural environment, in the heart of the tropical rainforests of the Western Ghats.

The Indian elephant, smaller than its African cousin, plays an essential role in the region's ecosystem. As "natural landscapers", they modify their habitat by creating clearings, thus facilitating the growth of new plants. Protecting these elephants is vital, as they are threatened by habitat loss due to deforestation and human expansion.

The Periyar sanctuary is home to over 1,000 elephants, making it the largest concentration of wild elephants in Asia. Eco-friendly safaris are organized to enable visitors to observe these animals in their natural habitat. Periyar is also a model of conservation, implementing initiatives to protect elephants from poaching and minimize conflicts between elephants and local people.

The elephant, sacred in Indian culture and often associated with the god Ganesh, is the object of special respect. In India, the elephant is not only a religious symbol, but also an integral part of daily life. Festivities and ceremonies are organized in their honor, particularly in the south of the country, where they are often decorated for parades.

Periyar's ecological and cultural importance makes it an essential step in the protection of Indian elephants. Thanks to conservation efforts and the involvement of local communities, this sanctuary is helping to preserve these emblematic animals for future generations.

Fact 55 - Raksha Bandhan, a festival celebrating fraternal ties

Raksha Bandhan is an iconic Indian festival celebrating the special bond between brothers and sisters. Literally, "Raksha" means protection and "Bandhan" means bond. On this festival, the sister ties a rakhi, a sacred thread, around her brother's wrist, symbolizing her prayer for his protection. In return, the brother promises to watch over her and protect her throughout her life. This simple but symbolic act strengthens family ties in many Indian communities.

The celebration of Raksha Bandhan dates back to ancient times and is mentioned in several Indian legends. For example, in the Mahabharata, Draupadi is said to have tied a piece of cloth around Krishna's wrist to dress a wound. In return, Krishna promised to protect her at all times. These mythological tales are often used to remind us of the importance of mutual protection between loved ones.

What makes this holiday unique is that it's not limited to the biological relationship between siblings. Close friends, cousins and even unrelated people can exchange rakhis. In this way, Raksha Bandhan becomes a moment of unity and solidarity beyond family boundaries. Women sometimes offer a rakhi to important protective figures in their lives, creating relationships of spiritual "brotherhood".

In addition to rakhi, gifts are often exchanged between brothers and sisters. The brother usually offers a gift in return, which may be symbolic or precious, depending on the means. It's a way of showing gratitude for the bond that unites them. The festivities are accompanied by family meals, sweets and warm moments of sharing.

This festival, celebrated throughout India, transcends cultural and religious differences. Whether in vast metropolises or remote villages, Raksha Bandhan reinforces the values of love, protection and unity, reminding us each year of the importance of family ties in Indian society.

Fact 56 - The Western Ghats are teeming with biodiversity

The Western Ghats, a mountain range along India's west coast, is considered one of the most biodiverse regions in the world. Listed as a UNESCO World Heritage Site, these mountains are home to an impressive variety of flora and fauna, much of which is endemic, i.e. found nowhere else. More than 7,400 plant species thrive here, of which around 1,800 are specific to this region, providing an exceptional ecosystem.

The biodiversity of the Western Ghats extends far beyond plants. The region is also home to over 500 species of freshwater fish, 225 species of amphibians, and over 400 species of butterflies, contributing to a crucial ecological balance. Creatures such as the Asiatic lion, the Indian elephant and the Bengal tiger find refuge in the dense forests of the Ghats, making it a natural sanctuary for some of India's most emblematic species.

This mountain range also plays a vital role in regulating the local climate. Thanks to its thick forests and numerous rivers, the Western Ghats influence the region's rainfall, creating microclimates that benefit the surrounding agriculture. These mountains act as a natural barrier to monsoon winds, capturing moisture and ensuring a water supply for the plains.

Despite their ecological importance, the Western Ghats face many threats, including deforestation, urbanization and the exploitation of natural resources. Various conservation programs have been set up to protect the region, and efforts are being made to promote sustainable development that respects the fragility of the ecosystem while enabling local communities to prosper.

The Western Ghats are a natural treasure trove that continues to fascinate scientists and nature lovers alike. Their unique biodiversity makes them an essential study site for conservation research, while attracting visitors from all over the world eager to discover the beauty and biological diversity of this extraordinary region.

Fact 57 - The Victoria Memorial, a vestige of colonial India

The Victoria Memorial, located in Kolkata, is one of the most striking symbols of the British colonial era in India. Built between 1906 and 1921, it was erected as a tribute to Queen Victoria after her death in 1901. Its impressive architecture, a blend of Victorian and Mughal styles, makes this monument a striking example of the fusion of cultures at a time when the British Empire was exerting its influence over the Indian subcontinent.

The monument is built of white marble, reminiscent of the Taj Mahal, and extends over 26 hectares of beautifully landscaped gardens. Dominated by a large central dome, the Victoria Memorial is flanked by several pavilions and surrounded by vast green gardens. It stands as a symbol of Britain's imperial power, but also as a reflection of Indian aesthetics through its local architectural influences.

Inside, the Victoria Memorial houses a museum with valuable collections tracing the history of British rule in India. Colonial artifacts, paintings, manuscripts and photographs document the period of the British Raj. These exhibits enable visitors to better understand the impact of colonization on India, as well as the relationship between India and Great Britain at that time.

Despite its roots in a controversial colonial past, the Victoria Memorial remains a popular site for tourists and locals alike, who come to admire its architecture, stroll through its gardens or explore its museum. Today, it is an integral part of Kolkata's cultural heritage, recalling both India's colonial history and its transition to independence.

The story of the Victoria Memorial illustrates the complexity of India's past, where British influence left lasting traces in architecture, art and society. This monument bears witness to a bygone era, while providing a space for reflection on India's rich and diverse history, shaped by multiple influences.

Fact 58 - India is the world's largest mango producer

India is the world's largest producer of mangoes, accounting for almost half of global production. The mango, often referred to as India's "king of fruits", is grown throughout the country, with regions such as Uttar Pradesh, Andhra Pradesh and Maharashtra leading the way in production. India's warm, humid climate is ideal for growing this fruit tree, which is an integral part of the country's culture and cuisine.

The country produces a wide variety of mangoes, including the famous Alphonso, Banganapalli and Dasheri. Each variety has a specific flavor, texture and color that appeal to mango lovers the world over. Alphonso, in particular, is renowned for its intense sweetness and unique aroma, making it one of the most prized varieties, both locally and abroad.

Mangoes play an important role in Indian culinary traditions. They are eaten fresh, made into chutneys, or used in savory dishes such as curries. Mango lassi, a mixture of mango and yoghurt, is one of the most popular drinks in summer to beat the heat. Mangoes are also dried for year-round consumption.

This fruit has not only economic importance, but also symbolic significance in Indian culture. Mango is often used in religious ceremonies and festivities. For example, mango leaves are hung on doors during certain festivals to symbolize prosperity and good luck.

With its vast production and cultural importance, the mango is much more than just a fruit in India. It embodies both the abundance of Indian nature and the country's deep attachment to its agricultural traditions, which nourish both bodies and souls.

Fact 59 - India's Constitution is one of the longest in the world

The Indian Constitution, adopted in 1950, is one of the longest in the world. It contains nearly 145,000 words in 448 articles, 12 annexes and over 100 amendments. It was drafted by the Indian Constituent Assembly, led by Dr. B. R. Ambedkar, after nearly three years of deliberation. This fundamental text embodies the aspirations of a young and diverse nation, just emerging from British colonial rule.

One of the most remarkable aspects of the Indian Constitution is its ability to take into account the country's linguistic, religious and cultural diversity. As a multilingual and multi-ethnic nation, India needed a legal framework capable of accommodating this plurality. This is why the Constitution grants specific protections to the various minorities and includes provisions to ensure equality before the law and the protection of the fundamental rights of all citizens.

This complex document deals with many aspects of public and governmental life, from fundamental rights to the structure of government, legislative and executive powers, and relations between the Union and the States. Its ambition is to guarantee stable democratic governance while ensuring social justice, equality and freedom for every citizen.

One of the interesting Facts about the Indian Constitution is its influence from constitutions around the world. For example, it draws on the British model for the parliamentary system, the US Constitution for fundamental rights and the separation of powers, and the Canadian system for federal relations between the central government and the states.

Even today, India's Constitution continues to adapt to the country's social, political and economic changes. The many amendments that have enriched it over the years are proof of its flexibility and relevance to the contemporary challenges of a democracy as vast and complex as India.

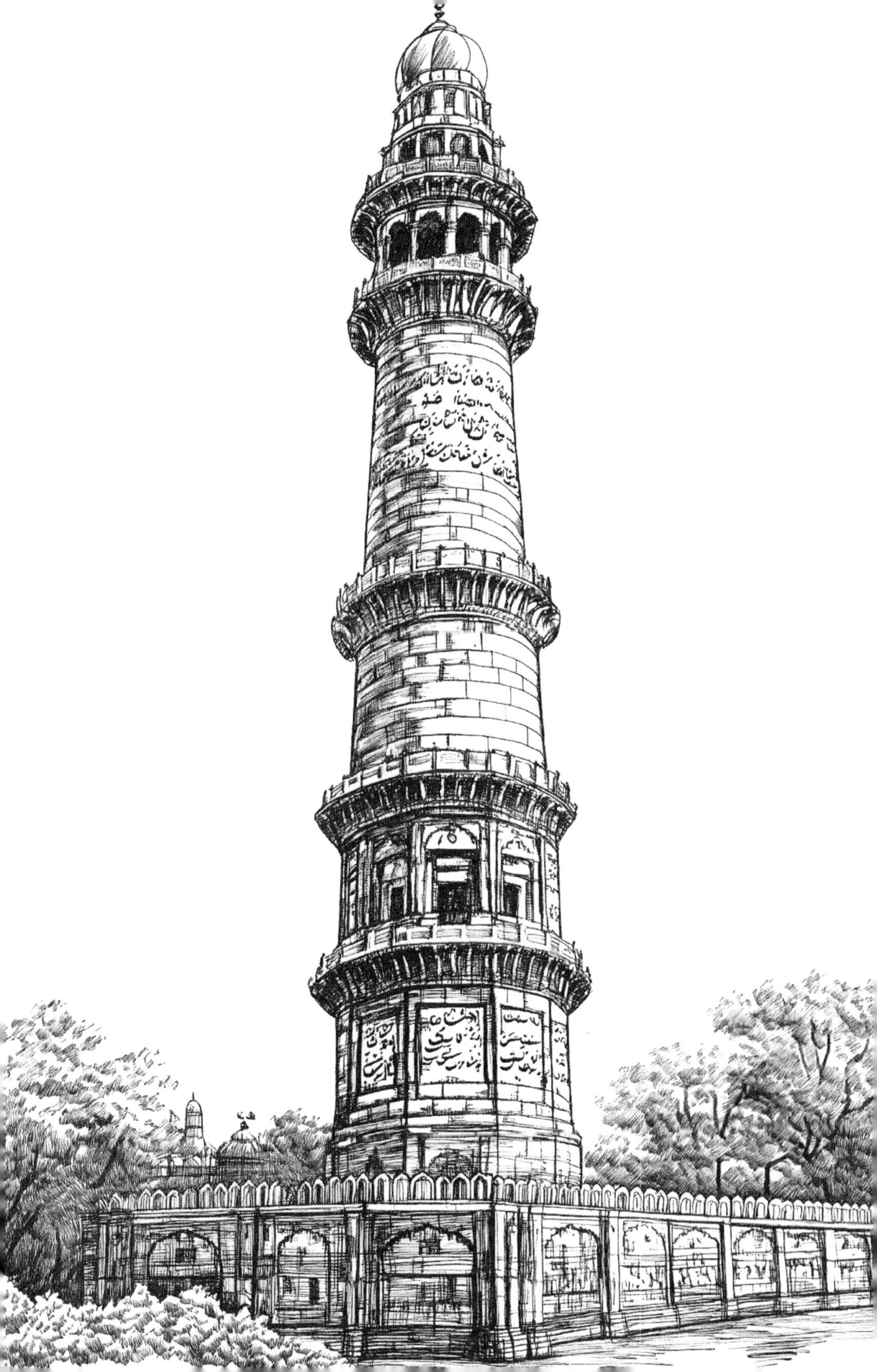

Fact 60 - The Qûtb Minâr tower, India's tallest minaret

The Qûtb Minâr in Delhi is India's tallest brick minaret, standing 73 metres high. Built in the early 13th century by Qûtb al-Dîn Aibak, the first Sultan of Delhi, it is an impressive symbol of Islamic architecture in India. With its five storeys, this imposing tower is made of red sandstone and adorned with intricate inscriptions in Arabic calligraphy, celebrating the glory of the rulers who built and enlarged it.

This historic monument is part of the Qûtb complex, a UNESCO World Heritage Site, and attracts visitors from all over the world fascinated by its height and architectural details. The tower consists of five distinct levels, each separated by balconies. Its diameter at the base is 14.3 metres, but shrinks to 2.7 metres at the top, creating a majestic elevation overlooking the surrounding area.

A fascinating Fact about the Qûtb Minâr is that it was inspired by Afghan minarets, notably that of Jam, but is unique in its size and materials. Its primary purpose was to serve as a victory tower, symbolizing the supremacy of the new Muslim rulers in India, while also fulfilling the function of a minaret to call the faithful to prayer in the adjacent mosque, Quwwat-ul-Islam.

Construction of the Qûtb Minâr was not completed by Qûtb al-Dîn Aibak himself. His successor, Shamsuddin Iltutmish, added three more floors, and later still, after lightning damage, Firoz Shah Tughlaq restored it and added the top floor. Thus, this tower symbolizes not only an initial victory, but also the evolution of the Delhi Sultan dynasty.

Today, the Qûtb Minâr remains an imposing witness to the history of India and its varied influences, blending local traditions with elements of Islamic architecture. It's a must-see for those wishing to immerse themselves in India's medieval history, while admiring a unique architectural masterpiece.

Fact 61 - More than 1,600 languages spoken in India

India is one of the most linguistically diverse countries in the world, with over 1600 languages spoken. This incredible diversity reflects the cultural and historical richness of the Indian subcontinent, where each region often has its own languages, dialects and variants. Of these languages, 22 are officially recognized by the Indian Constitution, such as Hindi, Bengali, Tamil and Telugu, but hundreds more are spoken in smaller communities.

This linguistic plurality is the result of centuries of migration, invasion, trade and cultural development. For example, in the northern regions of India, Indo-European languages dominate, while in the south, Dravidian languages such as Tamil and Kannada are widely spoken. Each language has its own history and reflects the identity of the community that speaks it, creating a unique cultural mosaic.

India's languages are not limited to national or regional ones. Tribal languages, spoken by indigenous groups in remote areas, also represent a valuable part of the country's linguistic heritage. These languages, though often threatened with extinction, are protected and documented by various efforts, both governmental and private, to preserve this wealth.

India is also a place where several languages often coexist in the same region or even within a family. It's not uncommon for a person to be fluent in several languages, such as Hindi for national interactions, English for business and a regional language for local exchanges. This multilingualism is a major asset in such a vast and varied country, facilitating communication across different regions.

In addition to the languages spoken, India uses several distinct writing systems. For example, Devanagari is used for Hindi and Marathi, while other languages, such as Bengali, Tamil and Gujarati, have their own alphabets. This linguistic diversity makes India a veritable cultural kaleidoscope, with each language contributing to the country's identity and richness.

Fact 62 - Basmati rice has a uniquely distinctive fragrance

Basmati rice, grown mainly in the northern regions of India and Pakistan, is renowned the world over for its distinct, delicate aroma. Its very name, "basmati", means "fragrant" in Hindi, and this rice is renowned for its subtle, floral fragrance that sets it apart from other rice varieties. This unique fragrance comes naturally from a chemical compound called 2-acetyl-1-pyrroline, present in greater quantities in basmati than in any other rice variety.

The cultivation of basmati rice is deeply rooted in Indian farming traditions, particularly in the fertile plains of the Himalayas, where the rich climate and soil contribute to its exceptional quality. Basmati is often preferred for preparing traditional dishes such as biryani, a blend of rice and spices, or pulao, where its fragrance beautifully complements the flavors of the ingredients.

One of the characteristics of basmati rice is its light, fluffy texture after cooking. Unlike other types of rice, which can become sticky, basmati remains well separated, offering a refined yet pleasant culinary experience. This lightness and its elongated grain make it an ingredient of choice in Indian cuisine, where it is often served with curries or dishes rich in sauces.

Basmati rice is also prized for its nutritional benefits. Although naturally low in fat, it is rich in carbohydrates, making it an ideal source of energy. Wholegrain basmati varieties also contain fiber, making it a nutritious food for a balanced diet.

The unique aroma and incomparable qualities of basmati rice make it a sought-after product far beyond India's borders. Thanks to its worldwide reputation, basmati is exported to many countries, reinforcing India's position as one of the world's leading producers and exporters of this precious variety of rice.

Fact 63 - The Silk Roads passed through India

The Silk Roads, that vast network of trade routes linking East and West, crossed India for centuries, playing a crucial role in the exchange of goods, cultures and ideas. These routes linked China to Europe, via Central Asia, and India played a central role thanks to its strategic geographical location. In addition to silk, India exported spices, precious stones, cotton and textiles - products prized throughout the ancient world.

The Indus valley and the Ganges plain, as well as cities like Taxila and Pataliputra, were major crossing points. India was more than just a commercial crossroads. Indian merchants brought with them craft innovations, such as textile dyeing, and products like pepper, which were particularly in demand in the West. Trade not only enriched the Indian economy, but also transformed daily life in India by introducing outside influences.

In addition to material goods, the Silk Roads also served as vectors for cultural and religious exchange. Travelers such as Buddhist monks used these routes to spread Buddhism throughout Central Asia and as far as China. In this way, the Silk Roads enabled India to spread its spiritual and philosophical teachings, in particular through famous centers of learning such as Nalanda.

Indian art and architecture were also enriched by these exchanges, incorporating Persian, Greek and Chinese influences. In return, Indian culture left its mark on the regions it passed through. This demonstrates the importance of the Silk Roads not only for the economy, but also for the cultural development of India and Asia.

Today, the vestiges of these routes can still be seen in monuments, ancient cities and historical accounts, testifying to India's importance in these global exchanges. These routes, much more than trade routes, were bridges linking civilizations, knowledge and cultures, with India as a key player in this rich global history.

Fact 64 - The forests of the Western Ghats are teeming with biodiversity

The Western Ghats, a mountain range along India's west coast, are one of the world's biodiversity gems. These mountains are home to a unique ecosystem, recognized by UNESCO as a World Heritage Site. The tropical rainforests that cover much of the Western Ghats are home to thousands of species of plants and animals, many of which are endemic to this region, i.e. found nowhere else in the world.

One of the outstanding features of this region is the diversity of its wildlife. It is home to iconic animals such as the Indian elephant and the Bengal tiger, as well as endangered species such as the Asiatic lion and the lion-tailed macaque. The Western Ghats play a vital role in the conservation of these species, offering a safe habitat away from human pressures. This wealth of biodiversity attracts not only biologists and researchers, but nature lovers from all over the world.

The forests of the Western Ghats are more than just remarkable wildlife. They are also a paradise for botanists. With over 7,000 listed plant species, many of which are used in traditional medicine, the flora of this region is of crucial importance to local populations. Medicinal herbs, fruit trees and rare plants play a fundamental role in the culture and economy of the indigenous communities living in these mountains.

What's more, the Western Ghats are essential to South India's climate regulation. These mountains capture moisture from monsoon winds, feeding rivers and lakes that provide fresh water for millions of people. The ecological role of this mountain range goes far beyond biodiversity, as it ensures the survival of numerous populations thanks to its water resources.

The Western Ghats are a natural treasure trove for India and the world. Their preservation is crucial not only for the species that live there, but also for maintaining the region's environmental balance.

Fact 65 - India invented the samosa, a tasty snack

Samosa, world-famous for its triangular shape and delicious taste, has its roots in India. This crunchy snack, often stuffed with spicy potatoes, peas or meat, is now a staple of quick meals and snacks across India. Its origins date back several centuries, and it is thought to have been introduced by merchants and travellers from the Middle East. However, India has made samosa an iconic dish by adapting it to its local tastes.

The modern version of samosa, mainly vegetarian, is extremely popular on Indian streets. Whether in small shops or on special occasions, you'll find this snack served with spicy and sweet chutneys. The complex and varied flavors it offers are a true representation of India's culinary diversity. It's also easy to prepare, making it widely accessible and appreciated by all.

Samosa has also evolved to reflect regional particularities. For example, in northern India it is generally larger and spicier, while in the west it is sometimes smaller and served with a variety of chutneys. The use of different spices, herbs and garnishes allows each region to reinvent this traditional dish according to its own preferences.

In addition to its place in everyday cooking, samosa is often served at festivals, weddings and other celebrations in India. It is seen as a symbol of conviviality and sharing. Whether served as a starter or a main course, it is a much-appreciated delicacy on every occasion, and continues to delight local and international palates alike.

Today, samosa has transcended India's borders to become a world-famous snack. Whether enjoyed in Asia, Europe or elsewhere, this dish reflects the ability of Indian cuisine to offer unique flavors and travel across cultures, while remaining true to its origins.

Fact 66 - Dholes are incredibly intelligent hunters

The dhole, also known as the Asian wild dog, is a fearsome and highly intelligent predator. Mainly found in India, this animal stands out for its sophisticated hunting techniques and ability to cooperate in packs. Indeed, dholes are renowned for their remarkable social organization, enabling them to hunt prey much larger than themselves, such as deer or wild boar.

Dholes never hunt alone. They strategize as a group, surrounding and isolating their target with impressive coordination. Their communication is equally fascinating: instead of barking like other canids, they use whistles, whines and even chirps to coordinate with each other. This subtle interaction enables them to adapt their tactics to suit the situation.

Their intelligence and agility make them highly efficient hunters. Unlike other predators, dholes can pursue their prey over long distances, using the pack's endurance to tire the animal out. Their hunting success is often linked to their unfailing cooperation, making dholes a perfect example of collective hunting in the animal kingdom.

Despite their intelligence and efficiency, dholes are unfortunately under threat. Deforestation and the reduction of their natural habitat in India are posing serious problems to their survival. Their numbers have declined in recent decades, and conservation efforts are now underway to protect this unique species.

In Indian culture, dholes are often viewed with fascination due to their astute behavior and ability to adapt to varied environments. They play an essential role in the ecosystem, regulating herbivore populations in forests and grasslands, and are a shining example of India's rich wildlife.

Fact 67 - The Sundarbans are home to hundreds of animal species

The Sundarbans, on the border between India and Bangladesh, form the world's largest mangrove swamp and are a veritable biodiversity sanctuary. These dense forests, covering more than 10,000 km², are home to an extremely rich and diverse fauna. Emblematic species such as the Bengal tiger, saltwater crocodiles and freshwater dolphins all coexist in this unique environment.

Sundarbans tigers, famed for their excellent swimming skills, represent one of the few tiger populations to have adapted to an aquatic habitat. However, these majestic felines are not the only predators in this ecosystem. Marine crocodiles, some reaching up to six meters in length, patrol the brackish waters, stalking their prey in the silence of rivers and canals.

The unique Sundarbans landscape provides ecological niches for a multitude of bird species, including kingfishers and herons. There is also a wide variety of mammals, reptiles, fish and insects. This complex network of interactions between species contributes to the richness of this ecosystem, which is essential for regulating animal populations.

In addition to large predators, the Sundarbans mangroves are also home to many endangered species. Sea turtles, pangolins and certain species of crabs and shrimps thrive here, benefiting from the abundance of natural resources. The dense forest, with its submerged roots, serves not only as a habitat, but also as a breeding ground for these animals.

The role of the Sundarbans goes beyond simple wildlife conservation. These forests act as a natural bulwark against cyclones and coastal erosion, while at the same time filtering water to protect the human populations living nearby. Their preservation is therefore essential, not only for the species that live there, but also for the local communities who depend on this unique ecosystem for their survival.

Fact 68 - The Deccan Plateau, one of the world's oldest formations

The Deccan Plateau in southern India is one of the world's oldest geological formations. Formed over 60 million years ago, this vast plateau extends over some 1.5 million square kilometers, covering much of central and southern India. Its volcanic origin makes it a unique area, marked by solidified lava flows that have given rise to a landscape of fertile, undulating land.

The Deccan plateau is framed by two mountain ranges: the Western Ghats to the west and the Eastern Ghats to the east. These mountains help to isolate the region, influencing its dry climate and rugged terrain. The mineral-rich volcanic soils have enabled the development of flourishing agriculture in certain areas, favoring the cultivation of cotton, sugarcane and cereals, essential to the local economy.

The importance of the Deccan Plateau goes beyond its geological aspect. This region was the scene of several ancient civilizations, including the Maurya and Chalukya empires, which shaped Indian history and culture. The black basalt rocks typical of the plateau were used to build numerous temples and forts, including the famous Daulatabad fort, a testament to the region's rich history.

The Deccan Plateau is also home to a unique flora and fauna. Although the region is characterized by an arid climate, it is home to several important nature reserves, such as the Tadoba-Andhari Reserve, home to endangered species such as the tiger. The dry forests and savannahs of the Deccan provide a vital ecosystem for a wide variety of plant and animal species.

Today, the Deccan Plateau remains a symbol of India's geological and historical richness. Its ancient character, rugged terrain and thriving cultures illustrate the close relationship between natural landscapes and the evolution of human societies in India.

Fact 69 - Hyderabad's iconic Charminar

The Charminar, located in the heart of Hyderabad, is one of India's most emblematic monuments. Built in 1591 by Sultan Muhammad Quli Qutb Shah, it celebrates the founding of Hyderabad and was also erected to mark the end of a devastating plague epidemic. This monument, at the crossroads of several historic routes, is a perfect example of Indo-Islamic architecture with Persian influences.

The name Charminar means "four minarets", in reference to the four majestic towers that rise from each corner of the monument. Each minaret is around 56 metres high, offering a panoramic view of the old city of Hyderabad. The entire structure, built in granite and limestone, is decorated with sculpted details, underlining the refinement of the art of the period.

Beyond its architecture, the Charminar is surrounded by a rich cultural history. It's close to the Mecca Masjid, one of India's largest mosques, and the Laad Bazaar market, famous for its lacquer bangles and traditional jewelry. The area surrounding the Charminar has always been a hub of commerce and culture in Hyderabad, attracting visitors from all over the world.

The Charminar has become a symbol of the city and a focal point for the people of Hyderabad. It is particularly lively during religious festivals such as Eid, when thousands of people gather around the monument to celebrate. Its central location and historical importance make it both a spiritual and social landmark.

Today, the Charminar remains a testament to the legacy of the Qutb Shahi sultans and a symbol of unity for Hyderabad. Its timeless charm attracts millions of tourists every year, while remaining a living landmark for local residents. The monument continues to captivate with its architectural beauty and historical significance, deeply rooted in Indian history.

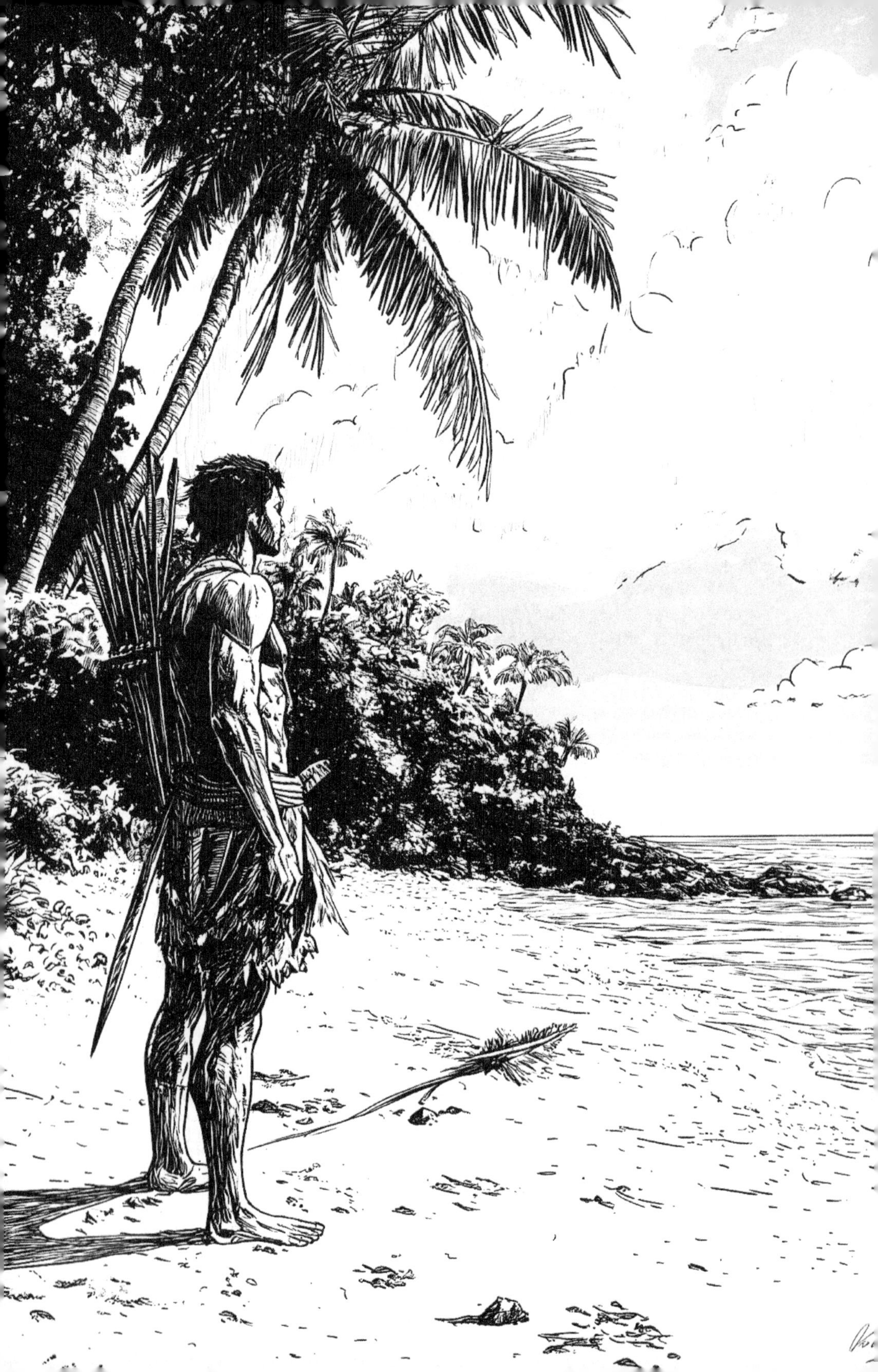

Fact 70 - Andaman tribes are among the most isolated in the world

The Andaman Islands in the Indian Ocean are home to some of the world's most isolated tribes. Among them, the Jarawas and the Sentinels, living in relative autarky, have managed to maintain their ancestral way of life for thousands of years. The Sentinels, in particular, are known to avoid all outside contact, firmly resisting modern intrusion on their island, North Sentinel Island.

These Andaman tribes live mainly from hunting, fishing and gathering, using traditional techniques handed down from generation to generation. The Sentinelese, for example, are renowned for their mastery of the bow and arrow, which they use to defend their territory against all outsiders, including attempts by the Indian government to contact them. Their way of life remains an enigma to the outside world, as they have never integrated modern practices.

The isolation of these tribes is largely due to the geography of the Andaman archipelago, which is far from India's main coastline. This natural distance, coupled with the tribes' desire to remain separate, has enabled these groups to preserve their unique customs. It is forbidden by Indian law to interact with some of these tribes in order to protect their culture and way of life. The Indian authorities have taken strict measures to prohibit any intrusion into their territories, particularly on North Sentinel Island.

The survival of these tribes in the face of the growing influence of the outside world is a testament to human diversity and cultural resilience. They offer a rare window on a way of life preserved since prehistoric times, although their future is fragile in the face of pressure from the modern world. Despite these challenges, the Presidia continue to defend their territory with impressive tenacity, underlining their fierce desire to remain independent from the rest of the world.

The case of the Andaman tribes, in particular the Presidia, fascinates researchers and defenders of indigenous rights. Their way of life, so far removed from modern standards, reminds us that certain human groups, though rare, still have the choice to preserve their isolation in an increasingly connected world.

Fact 71 - Ganesh Chaturthi, celebrated with giant statues

Ganesh Chaturthi is one of India's most popular religious festivals, dedicated to the god Ganesh, known for his elephant head and his role as "deflector of obstacles". Each year, this celebration is marked by the creation and procession of giant statues of Ganesh, which are installed in temples and homes, carefully decorated and worshipped for several days before being immersed in a river or the ocean. These statues can measure up to several dozen meters in height.

The origins of this festival go back thousands of years, but it was in the 19th century that Ganesh Chaturthi took on its modern stature, largely thanks to Bal Gangadhar Tilak, a leader of Indian independence. He saw the festival as a means of uniting Indians under British rule, making Ganesh Chaturthi a symbol of unity and peaceful resistance. Today, it is celebrated all over India, but particularly in Mumbai and Pune, where parades of colossal statues attract huge crowds.

The process of creating the statues is an art in itself. Made mainly of clay, they are painted and decorated in bright colors. These statues, small or huge, are meticulously sculpted by craftsmen who sometimes spend months making them. Families and communities gather to offer prayers and songs to Ganesh, asking for blessings, success and prosperity.

The ten-day festivities culminate in a ritual known as "Visarjan", when the statues are carried in a vibrant, colorful procession to a body of water for immersion. This moment symbolizes Ganesh's departure for his heavenly abode, while bringing good fortune and peace to those who have worshipped him. It's also a moment of collective emotion, when millions of devotees follow the procession, singing and dancing to bid farewell to their beloved deity.

The importance of Ganesh Chaturthi transcends religion. The festival is a celebration of culture, unity and creativity. The giant Ganesh statues, an impressive sight, attract visitors from all over the world, and reflect the artistic and spiritual richness of India.

Fact 72 - Navratri celebrates the victory of good over evil

Navratri is one of India's most important festivals, celebrating the victory of good over evil over nine nights. The name "Navratri" comes from Sanskrit and means "nine nights". During this period, Hindus pay homage to the goddess Durga, who embodies divine feminine strength and triumph over the demon Mahishasura. Each day of the festival is dedicated to a specific form of the goddess, marking a spiritual journey of purification and renewal.

The legend behind Navratri tells how Durga, after nine days of battle, defeated Mahishasura, a powerful demon who sowed chaos. This victory symbolizes the destruction of evil forces and the establishment of cosmic order. It is also a metaphor for the inner struggle to overcome one's own demons and get through life's trials.

Navratri is celebrated differently in different parts of India. In the state of Gujarat, for example, people dance the Garba, a circular dance in tribute to the goddess, while in West Bengal, Durga Puja, another form of Navratri, is marked by giant statues of Durga decorated and immersed in water at the end of the celebrations. Each region thus puts forward its own cultural and artistic interpretation of this festival, while remaining faithful to its spiritual essence.

In addition to dances and rituals, Navratri is also a period of fasting and prayer. Believers often choose to forgo certain foods or follow a special diet for these nine days. The purpose of this fast is to purify the body and mind, while strengthening devotion and spiritual concentration. Temples and homes are decorated with lights and flowers, creating an atmosphere of festivity and devotion.

The importance of Navratri goes beyond mythology. It's a celebration of the power of goodness and the courage needed to face hardship. The festival brings together millions of people who, for nine days, connect with their spiritual and cultural roots, while celebrating the unity and diversity of India through its varied customs and rituals.

Fact 73 - Jaisalmer Fort, a citadel in the desert

The fort of Jaisalmer, nicknamed the "Golden Citadel", stands majestically in the heart of the Thar Desert, in the state of Rajasthan. The fort is one of the oldest and most impressive in India, built in the 12th century by Rawal Jaisal, a Rajput king. Built of yellow sandstone, it gleams like gold in the sunlight, creating a striking contrast with the vast arid expanses that surround it.

This citadel is not only a military monument, but also a living city. Thousands of people still live, work and trade here today. The fort boasts royal palaces, beautifully carved Jain temples and houses, all linked by winding lanes. This blend of defensive architecture and urban life makes it a unique example of inhabited fortification.

Historically, the fort of Jaisalmer was a strategic trading point, as it lay on the ancient caravan routes linking India to the Middle East and Central Asia. Merchants carried spices, silk and precious stones across these routes, contributing to the city's wealth and prosperity. This commercial role has left its mark on the fort's architecture, with its havelis (merchants' houses) adorned with carved balconies.

The fort has also seen several sieges and battles in its history, notably against Mughal armies. Despite these attacks, it was never totally destroyed, remaining a symbol of the rajputs' resilience and determination to protect their land. Its elevated position on a hill made it easy to monitor enemy movements in the surrounding desert.

Today, Jaisalmer Fort is a UNESCO World Heritage Site and continues to attract visitors from all over the world. Its panoramic views of the Thar Desert, combined with its historic atmosphere, make it a must-see destination for history and architecture enthusiasts, as well as a gateway to the ancient, rugged soul of Rajasthan.

Fact 74 - Yoga has its roots in sacred texts

Yoga, now practised the world over, has its origins in the sacred texts of ancient India, notably the Vedas and the Upanishads. These writings, which date back several millennia, already evoke the spiritual and philosophical foundations of yoga. They describe practices designed to harmonize body and mind, linking the individual to the universal. The word "yoga" comes from the Sanskrit "yuj", meaning "union", symbolizing the connection between body, mind and soul.

Among the founding texts, Patanjali's Yoga Sutras are particularly important. Written some 2,000 years ago, they contain 196 aphorisms that codify the practice of yoga. These aphorisms describe eight stages of yoga, ranging from moral disciplines (yama and niyama) to physical postures (asanas) and meditation techniques. Patanjali systematized these practices to make them accessible to all, showing that yoga was not simply a series of physical exercises, but a profound spiritual path.

The Upanishads, also considered sacred texts, mention meditation and breath control practices that are now an integral part of modern yoga. These practices were intended to awaken consciousness and lead to spiritual liberation (moksha). The Bhagavad Gita, another major sacred text, also describes various forms of yoga, such as Bhakti Yoga (yoga of devotion) and Karma Yoga (yoga of selfless action), emphasizing that yoga goes beyond physical postures alone.

Yoga has evolved over the centuries, but its foundation remains anchored in these ancient writings. These texts emphasize that yoga is a complete discipline, aiming to achieve balance between body, mind and universe. The physical postures we know today are only a small part of a larger system, in which meditation, breathing and ethics play a central role.

In India, these practices are still alive and well, and many yoga centers across the country perpetuate this heritage. Far from being just an exercise, yoga is a true philosophy of life, with roots that go deep into India's spiritual and cultural history.

Fact 75 - Sanskrit, one of the world's oldest languages

Sanskrit is one of the oldest languages known to mankind, with a history dating back over 3,500 years. Originating in India, this classical language has played a central role in the transmission of Indian knowledge and culture down the centuries. The oldest religious texts of Hinduism, the Vedas, are written in Vedic Sanskrit, a primitive dialect of the language dating from around 1500 BC. It is the language of sacred prayers, songs and hymns.

Sanskrit evolved over time, and around the first millennium BC, it took on a more standardized form known as classical Sanskrit. This version, codified by the famous grammarian Panini in his work "Ashtadhyayi", is a major work of world linguistics. Panini laid the foundations of Sanskrit grammar with astonishing precision, creating rules that remain relevant to this day. His work not only influenced the language, but also many other linguistic systems.

Sanskrit is not only a religious and philosophical language, but also a language of science, mathematics and poetry. Texts such as the Mahabharata, the Ramayana and the Upanishads, among the greatest treasures of world literature, were written in Sanskrit. These works continue to be studied and respected not only in India, but in academic centers the world over.

Although Sanskrit is no longer a common vernacular language today, it remains alive through religious rites, ceremonies and academic teaching. In India, many temples still use Sanskrit for rituals, and some schools teach this ancient language to preserve its rich heritage. It is also an important source for the comparative study of Indo-European languages.

Sanskrit has had a profound influence on India, not only through its role in religion and literature, but also as a vehicle for the transmission of scientific, philosophical and cultural knowledge. Even today, Sanskrit inspires and influences modern disciplines such as linguistics, mathematics and computer science.

Fact 76 - Asia's largest tulip garden in Kashmir

The Kashmir Tulip Garden in Srinagar is the largest in Asia. Nestled at the foot of the majestic Himalayan Mountains, this garden offers a dazzling spectacle in spring, when millions of tulips of different colors carpet the ground. Covering almost 30 hectares, it attracts visitors from all over the world to admire the beauty of its flowers, which form a multicolored carpet stretching as far as the eye can see.

Created in 2007, this garden, also known as the Indira Gandhi Memorial Tulip Garden, was designed to boost tourism in the Kashmir region. It quickly gained in popularity thanks to its enchanting setting and the diversity of the tulip varieties it houses. Each year, during the Tulip Festival, visitors can contemplate over 60 varieties of flowers, each adding a unique touch to the landscape.

This garden is not only a symbol of natural beauty, but also a testament to the region's rich biodiversity. In addition to tulips, it is surrounded by magnolias, narcissi and many other exotic plants, making it a veritable botanical paradise. The idyllic setting, with Lake Dal in the background, enhances the charm and serenity of the site, attracting tourists and nature lovers alike.

The Kashmir Tulip Garden is also an example of the resilience and optimism of the people of this often troubled region. Despite the difficulties, the beauty of this garden and the efforts to make it a major floral attraction testify to the desire to showcase Kashmir's natural splendor and encourage visitors back to the region.

Every spring, the garden becomes a place of celebration, where visitors can enjoy not only nature, but also the cultural traditions of the region, with local dance and music enlivening the festival. The Srinagar Tulip Garden is now a national pride and a unique floral treasure.

Fact 77 - The Himalayas influence India's climate

The Himalayas, an imposing mountain range stretching for thousands of kilometers, play an essential role in regulating India's climate. As a natural barrier, it prevents cold winds from Central Asia from penetrating the Indian subcontinent. As a result, India enjoys a warmer climate, even during the winter months, than other regions at the same latitude.

One of the Himalayas' most remarkable contributions to India's climate is its role in the monsoon phenomenon. By blocking moist winds from the Indian Ocean, it forces these air masses to rise and condense, resulting in heavy rainfall. This seasonal rainfall, which mainly affects the northern and eastern regions of India, is vital to the country's agriculture, nourishing the land and supporting millions of farmers.

The Himalayas influence more than just temperatures and rainfall. It also shapes atmospheric currents. During the summer months, the heat of the Indian plateau creates a depression that draws moisture-laden winds towards the country, contributing to the regularity of the monsoon. In winter, the Himalayas protect India's northern plains from extreme weather.

Rivers that originate in the Himalayas, such as the Ganges, Brahmaputra or Indus, also shape regional climates by regulating water availability throughout the year. These rivers influence the microclimate of the plains and regions they cross, and are essential to the irrigation and water needs of millions of people.

The Himalayas are not only a majestic mountain range, but also a key player in India's climatic equilibrium. Its effects can be seen in the daily lives of its inhabitants, from agricultural cycles to seasonal variations, making this natural barrier an indispensable element in understanding the sub-continent's climate.

Fact 78 - The Ganges is home to the freshwater dolphin

The sacred River Ganges, the artery of life in India, is home to a unique and fascinating species: the freshwater dolphin, also known as "Susu" in Hindi. This rare mammal, which lives only in the rivers of South Asia, is a symbol of the region's exceptional biodiversity. Unlike marine dolphins, the Ganges river dolphin is perfectly adapted to life in the fresh, muddy waters of major rivers such as the Ganges and Brahmaputra.

One of the most remarkable features of this dolphin is its near-blindness. Due to the often murky waters of the Ganges, it relies mainly on echolocation to move around and hunt. It emits sonic clicks that bounce off surrounding objects, enabling it to locate its prey and avoid obstacles. This adaptation is a fine example of how species evolve to survive in specific environments.

The Ganges river dolphin plays a crucial role in the river ecosystem. As a predator, it helps maintain the balance of fish populations and other aquatic species. However, this animal is now in danger, notably due to water pollution, overfishing and dams that fragment its natural habitat. Several initiatives have been launched to protect this species, including conservation programs and efforts to reduce river pollution.

In addition to its ecological importance, the freshwater dolphin has a profound cultural value in India. A symbol of purity and wisdom in certain local traditions, it is respected and protected by the people who live along the Ganges. Festivals and awareness campaigns are often organized to inform communities about the importance of its conservation.

So this rare and mysterious dolphin is much more than just an animal species. It embodies the profound link between the Ganges and the life it sustains, reminding us of the interdependence between river ecosystems and the human populations that depend on them.

Fact 79 - Himalayan rivers spring from millennia-old glaciers

The rivers of the Himalayas, among the most important in Asia, have their source in millennia-old glaciers at dizzying altitudes. The Ganges, Brahmaputra and Indus, emblematic rivers of India, are fed by the melting of these glacial masses. These glaciers, formed thousands of years ago, play a key role in the region's ecosystem, providing precious water for millions of people and rich biodiversity.

Himalayan glaciers, such as the Gangotri glacier from which the Ganges emerges, are essential for maintaining a constant supply of water, even during dry periods. Their slow melting feeds the rivers throughout the year, guaranteeing the survival of the populations living downstream, particularly in the fertile plains of northern India. This millennia-old natural cycle is at the heart of the region's agricultural and economic stability.

Over the centuries, these rivers have shaped not only landscapes, but also civilizations. Water flowing down from glaciers is considered sacred in many local cultures, particularly in Hinduism, where the Ganges is worshipped as a goddess. Glacial streams are also essential for irrigation, agriculture and the supply of drinking water, sustaining millions of human and animal lives.

Today, however, the Himalayan glaciers are under threat from climate change. Their accelerated melting endangers the equilibrium of rivers and increases the risk of flash floods, disrupting the lives of riverside communities. Conservation initiatives and scientific efforts are underway to understand and curb these phenomena. The melting of these glaciers could profoundly affect not only the Himalayas, but also the economies and ecosystems of regions much further afield.

Rivers born of Himalayan glaciers embody the power and fragility of nature. Their waters link isolated high-altitude regions with fertile plains, and carry with them a millennia-old heritage that is both a source of life and spiritual inspiration.

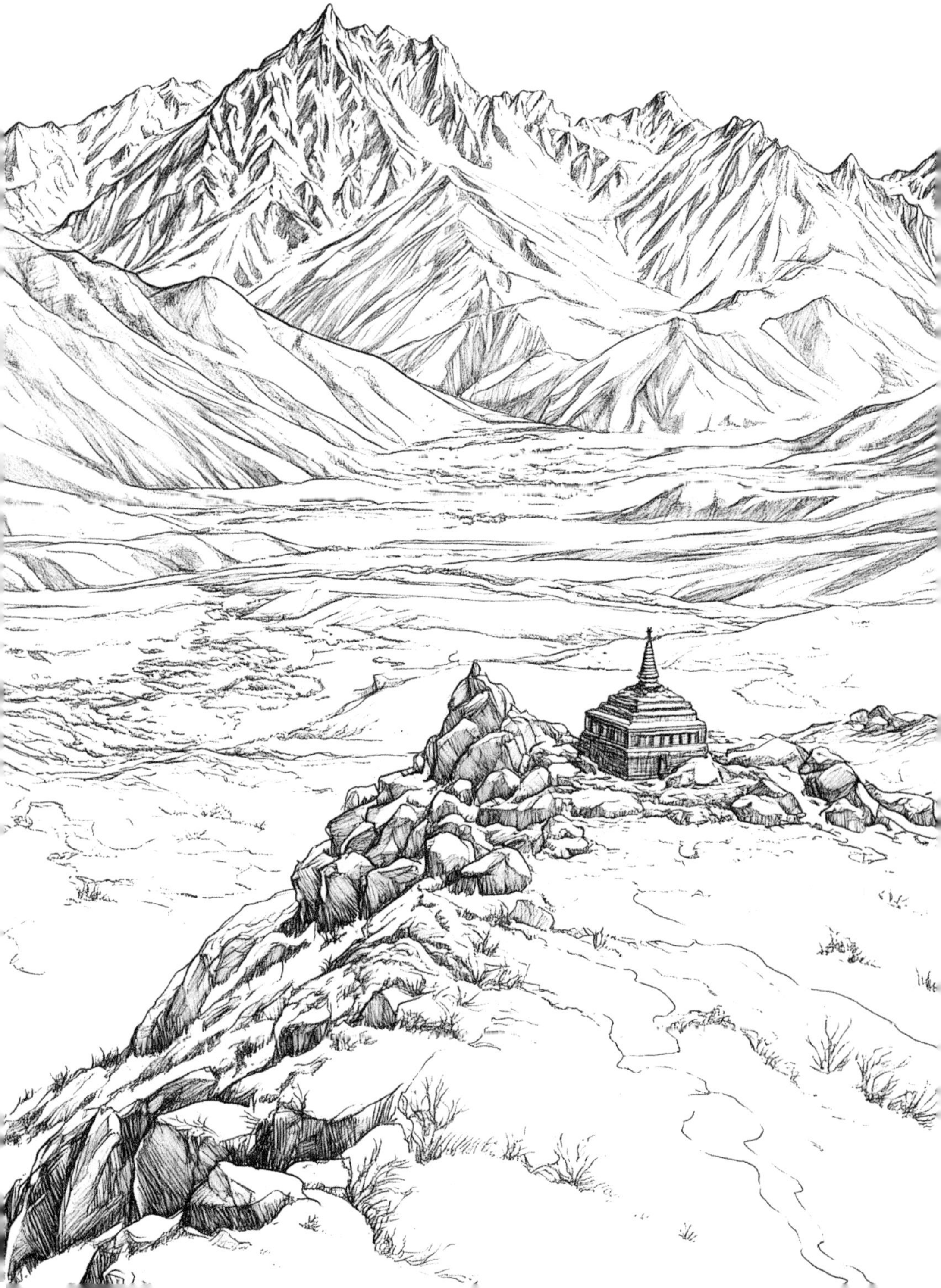

Fact 80 - Ladakh, famous for its icy desert landscapes

Ladakh, located in northern India, is a unique frozen desert perched at over 3,000 meters above sea level. Known for its arid mountains and spectacular valleys, it offers a striking contrast to other, often greener, regions of India. In winter, Ladakh is transformed into a land of ice, with temperatures dropping well below zero, accentuating its hostile desert aspect.

This region, bordered by the Himalayas and the Karakoram range, is crossed by numerous passes and icy rivers, such as the Indus, which rises here. Ladakh's lunar landscapes, with high-altitude lakes like Pangong Tso and windswept plateaus, attract travelers in search of solitude and awe in the face of raw nature. The snow-capped peaks that surround this region add an icy majesty to this already striking environment.

Ladakh is not only famous for its panoramic views, but also for its deep-rooted Tibetan Buddhist culture. Numerous hilltop monasteries, such as Thiksey or Hemis, are important spiritual centers. These holy places, often shrouded in snow, seem timeless and offer a peaceful atmosphere that contrasts with the harshness of the climate and terrain.

Despite its desert-like appearance, Ladakh is home to an astonishing biodiversity, including rare species such as the snow leopard and the wild Tibetan donkey, the kiang. This fauna has adapted to the region's extreme conditions, underlining the resilience of life in such an inhospitable environment. The inhabitants, mainly Ladakhis, share this endurance, living in isolated villages where resources are limited, but where culture and spirituality thrive.

Ladakh is often referred to as "Little Tibet", due to its geographical isolation and well-preserved Tibetan culture. This remote and mysterious territory, with its icy deserts and towering mountains, continues to fascinate and challenge those who venture there, offering them an encounter with both extreme nature and an age-old culture.

Fact 81 - The Yamuna is considered a sacred goddess

The Yamuna, one of India's largest rivers, is much more than just a watercourse for millions of Indians. It is revered as a sacred goddess, a symbol of purity and fertility in Hindu culture. The Yamuna is often associated with ancient legends and features in many mythological accounts, including that of the god Krishna, who is said to have spent much of his childhood near its banks, in Vrindavan.

Believers consider the Yamuna to be the daughter of the sun god, Surya, and the sister of Yama, the god of death. This divine filiation reinforces its sacred position and makes it a source of blessings. Throughout its course, the Yamuna is the object of numerous religious rituals, particularly during festivities such as the Chhath Puja, when devotees come to pray on its banks and place offerings to receive its grace.

Many holy cities, such as Agra and Mathura, lie along the banks of the Yamuna, further enhancing its spiritual importance. In Delhi, the Yamuna River is a source of cultural and religious life, although its ecological state poses challenges. For its inhabitants, it remains a key element of their spiritual identity, a link with deities and age-old traditions.

Despite the pollution problems affecting the Yamuna today, devotees continue to believe in its purifying power. Bathing in its waters is seen as an act of purification from sin and a means of attaining moksha, or spiritual liberation. This belief is rooted in the conviction that the goddess Yamuna can grant salvation to those who come to her with devotion.

The Yamuna thus embodies both a vital natural entity and a protective divine figure. This dual role makes it a powerful symbol of how nature and spirituality are intimately linked in Indian culture, transcending physical realities to enter the sacred dimension of Hindu beliefs.

Fact 82 - Sushruta, pioneer of plastic surgery in India

Sushruta, an ancient Indian physician, is considered the father of plastic surgery. His major work, the Sushruta Samhita, is a medical treatise detailing over 300 surgical procedures, including advanced reconstructive techniques, long before the emergence of modern medicine. In this way, he laid the foundations for reconstructive surgery, in particular for the repair of the nose, known today as rhinoplasty.

Probably living around the 6th century BC, Sushruta was renowned for his ability to treat war wounds and disfigurement. His method of nasal reconstruction was used for victims of punishments in which the nose was cut off. His technique involved using a piece of skin taken from the forehead, which he shaped to reshape the nose. This procedure is now recognized as a precursor of modern plastic surgery.

The Sushruta Samhita also deals with many other medical practices, including descriptions of Caesarean section, stone removal and even limb amputation. This fundamental text shows just how advanced medical knowledge was in India at the time. Sushruta also dealt with the preparation and use of surgical instruments, many of which were tailor-made for the type of operation to be performed.

Sushruta's teachings not only influenced Indian medicine, but crossed frontiers, reaching Middle Eastern civilizations and, later, Europe. Centuries after his time, his work continues to fascinate physicians and historians alike for the precision and sophistication of its techniques. His impact on the field of reconstructive surgery remains immeasurable.

Sushruta's fundamental contributions to surgery have left a lasting legacy. His innovations bear witness to ancient Indian medical ingenuity, and his name is honored today as that of a pioneer who transformed the way surgical reconstruction is approached around the world.

Fact 83 - The Silk Roads ran through India

The Silk Roads, famous for connecting East and West, also crossed India, playing an essential role in commercial and cultural exchanges between Asia and Europe. For centuries, these routes carried silk, precious stones, spices and other valuable goods across India's vast territories, linking India to China, Central Asia and the Mediterranean.

Thanks to their strategic location, Indian merchants were at the heart of these exchanges. India offered luxury goods such as spices, cotton and textiles, which were highly prized by the Roman and Byzantine empires. In return, India imported silk from China, as well as ideas, inventions and cultural influences that enriched its own heritage. The Silk Roads were therefore not only trade routes, but also vectors of cultural exchange.

Important Indian cities such as Taxila and Varanasi became crossroads of commerce and knowledge. Taxila, in particular, became a renowned center of learning, attracting scholars from all over the world, thus fostering the spread of religious and philosophical ideas, such as Buddhism. Buddhism, moreover, spread to China and Southeast Asia via these same trade routes, testifying to the impact of the Silk Roads on cultures and religions.

In addition to commercial and intellectual exchanges, these routes also facilitated political alliances between different civilizations. For example, the Maurya took advantage of these routes to establish diplomatic contacts with the Roman Empire and Persia. These connections not only strengthened local economies, but also enabled a constant flow of technological innovations, such as Indian mathematics and astronomy, which traveled along these routes.

The historical importance of the Silk Roads is undeniable. They shaped India's development as a global crossroads, linking civilizations, goods and ideas. Even today, their legacy can be seen in the traces left by these ancient trade routes, which continue to influence India's culture and heritage.

Fact 84 - Meghalaya's underground river remains a mystery

In the northeastern Indian state of Meghalaya lies one of nature's most mysterious wonders: an underground river winding through a vast network of limestone caves. This network, one of the longest and most complex in the world, is home to the Umngot River, which remains largely unexplored due to the difficulty of accessing some of its underground sections.

This region of Meghalaya is renowned for its unique karst landscapes, formed by centuries of erosion of limestone rock by underground water. Caves such as Siju Cave and Liat Prah Cave are famous not only for their beauty, but also for the enigmas they conceal. The Umngot River, with its crystal-clear waters, is famous for giving the illusion that boats float on air. However, its underground route remains largely an enigma, as explorations are limited by rugged geography and lack of data.

Beyond its mystery, this river is a precious source for the local ecosystem. It feeds the surrounding communities and supports a diverse fauna, while remaining in harmony with the dense forest that surrounds it. Explorers who have attempted to map the underground river network have often been surprised by the exceptional biodiversity hidden underground, including endemic fish species.

Local culture associates the river with ancient legends. For indigenous tribes, caves and underground rivers are sacred places, steeped in mysticism. Stories tell of the Umngot River as a spiritual pathway to hidden realms. This blend of nature and mystery continues to attract researchers and the curious who hope to unlock the secrets of these hidden waters beneath the earth.

The caves of Meghalaya, with their fascinating underground river, remain an invitation to explore. Although many sections remain unexplored, researchers continue to study this inhospitable region, in the hope of discovering more about this natural underground masterpiece that testifies to India's incredible geological diversity.

Fact 85 - The zero discovered by Indian mathematician Aryabhata

One of India's greatest contributions to the world is the discovery of the zero, made by the famous mathematician Aryabhata. Born in 476 A.D., Aryabhata is often recognized for his major advances in mathematics and astronomy. His understanding of zero was not just a numerical innovation, but a revolutionary concept that would transform calculus, science and even philosophy.

Before the discovery of the zero, civilizations used numerical systems without this notion, making certain calculations extremely complex. Aryabhata's work simplified mathematical methods, particularly in the fields of algebra and trigonometry. He used the zero as a distinct symbol in his calculations and developed equations based on this concept. This not only made mathematics easier, but also paved the way for major scientific discoveries.

The use of zero also had a profound influence on astronomy. Aryabhata, in his treatise "Aryabhatiya", used this concept to determine very precise astronomical calculations. Thanks to his understanding of equations and geometry, he was able to accurately measure the length of the solar year and address phenomena such as eclipses. His vision of the universe, underpinned by the use of zero, was already remarkably accurate for its time.

The impact of Aryabhata and zero spread far beyond India. Arab scholars subsequently adopted the concept, and passed it on to Europe through trade and cultural routes. The zero was integrated into Arab numerical systems, and then into the decimal system we still use today. This mathematical heritage, rooted in India, has shaped centuries of scientific progress around the world.

Zero is much more than just a number. It is a fundamental concept in science, technology and modern thought. This symbol, discovered by Aryabhata, has enabled mankind to perform calculations that would otherwise be impossible. It is proof of India's mathematical genius and the impact of this civilization on human knowledge.

Fact 86 - Monkeys protect temples in India

In India, certain temples are closely associated with monkeys, regarded as sacred protectors. These primates, often present in large numbers in the vicinity of such sites, are not seen as mere animals, but as beings linked to divinity, in particular Hanuman, the monkey-god of the Hindu pantheon. He is the embodiment of loyalty and strength, and his images are revered throughout the country, creating a spiritual link between the temples and the monkeys that inhabit them.

In places like the Galta Ji temple in Jaipur, or the Hanuman temple in Hampi, these monkeys have a special place. Visitors often come with offerings not only for the deities, but also to feed the animals. The monkeys reign supreme, moving freely around the temple grounds. Although they can sometimes seem mischievous, their presence is tolerated and often encouraged by the faithful.

The behavior of the monkeys in these temples shows their intelligence and developed habit of cohabitation with humans. Sometimes seen as guardians, they instinctively watch over the premises. This closeness to humans, combined with mutual respect, enables them to thrive in these sacred environments. Monkeys, particularly langurs and macaques, seem to understand the importance of these sites and behave differently than in other urban areas.

It's fascinating to see the extent to which mythology and religion play a role in the perception of animals in India. The veneration of Hanuman and the importance of monkeys in Hindu tradition elevate them to a quasi-divine status. Their relationship with temples reinforces this spiritual aspect, where the boundaries between the animal and human worlds blur to create a sacred interaction.

This harmonious coexistence between monkeys and temples is an example of Indian culture's deep attachment to nature and animals. It also shows how ancient beliefs still shape modern practices, where temples become refuges for these primates, both respected and protected by devotees.

Fact 87 - The Chambal River is home to rare crocodiles

The Chambal River, which flows through several states in northern India, is home to a remarkable aquatic fauna, including some of the rarest crocodile species in the world. Among them, the gharial, a long-snouted crocodile, is critically endangered. This reptile, unique in its appearance and feeding habits, finds refuge in the clear, unpolluted waters of the Chambal, one of the last natural habitats where it can still thrive.

The gharial is distinguished by its singular morphology: its long, tapering snout enables it to hunt fish, its main diet. Unlike other crocodile species, it poses no threat to humans, making it easy to coexist with local populations. The Chambal River has thus become a natural sanctuary for this species, protected by conservation efforts aimed at preserving this precious ecosystem.

In addition to the gharial, Chambal is also home to the more common but equally fascinating swamp crocodile. These crocodiles, capable of surviving in a variety of environments, share the territory with other emblematic species such as river dolphins and various freshwater turtles. The biodiversity that characterizes this region makes it an area of international importance for conservation.

Efforts to protect the crocodiles of the Chambal River have resulted in the establishment of a nature reserve: the Chambal Sanctuary. Created to combat poaching and habitat degradation, this sanctuary ensures the protection of these reptiles while raising awareness among local communities of the importance of preserving this natural heritage. The joint actions of the authorities and ecologists have led to a gradual increase in the gharial population, a major victory in the fight to preserve endangered species.

The Chambal River, with its crucial role in the preservation of rare crocodiles, symbolizes the delicate balance between nature and human actions. It is a reminder of the need for sustainable management of natural resources to protect India's unique biodiversity, where species such as the gharial can still thrive in their ancestral habitat.

Fact 88 - India has the world's largest postal network

India's postal network, known as India Post, is the largest in the world, with over 150,000 post offices spread across the country. This vast network stretches from major cities to the most remote villages, ensuring that every citizen, even in the most isolated regions, has access to postal services. This impressive infrastructure reflects the geographical and demographic diversity of India, where the mail plays an essential role in the daily lives of millions of people.

The history of India Post dates back to colonial times, when the British began structuring a postal system to link their administration across the subcontinent. Since then, the network has gone from strength to strength, becoming not only a means of communication for letters and parcels, but also a key player in rural development, offering banking, savings and even insurance services to remote populations.

One of the most fascinating aspects of this network is the diversity of the means used to convey mail. While in the big cities, letters circulate rapidly thanks to modern infrastructures, in mountainous regions or deserts, more traditional methods are still employed. For example, in certain regions of the Himalayas or Rajasthan, letter carriers use horses or even boats to reach remote villages.

India Post also holds some impressive records, such as that of the world's highest altitude post office. Located in Hikkim, in the state of Himachal Pradesh, this office stands at an altitude of over 4,400 meters, serving a mountain population that depends on the service for communications with the rest of the country. It is a testament to India Post's commitment to serving even the most remote areas.

India Post's role has evolved over time. Although the volume of physical mail has declined with the digital age, India's postal network remains vital to many Indians, particularly in rural areas. Thanks to its efforts to adapt to new technologies, India Post continues to play a crucial role in the country's connectivity, reinforcing its status as the world's largest postal network.

Fact 89 - Kangchenjunga, the world's third highest mountain

Kangchenjunga, located on the border between India and Nepal, is the third highest mountain in the world, culminating at 8,586 meters above sea level. Its name, of Tibetan origin, means "the five treasures of the great snow", in reference to its five main peaks. This majestic massif, often shrouded in cloud and mystery, occupies a sacred place in the culture and history of the local population, particularly the Sikkimese, who consider it the abode of a protective deity.

The mountain is part of the Himalayan range, and its Indian side is located in the state of Sikkim. Unlike Everest, which attracts crowds of climbers every year, Kangchenjunga has long been preserved from mass tourism due to its technical difficulty and local traditions. The people of Sikkim discourage full ascent of the summit out of respect for the mountain's sacred nature. As a result, even the first victorious expeditions stopped a few meters short of the summit out of deference to this belief.

The history of Kangchenjunga ascents is marked by both feats and tragedies. The first successful expedition dates back to 1955, led by British mountaineers Joe Brown and George Band. Since then, only a few experienced climbers have dared to take up the challenge, as the ascent is considered extremely dangerous. Steep slopes, frequent avalanches and unpredictable weather conditions make it one of the most difficult mountains in the world to conquer.

Kangchenjunga plays an essential role in the surrounding ecosystem. Glaciers extending from its peaks feed local rivers, providing a vital source of water for millions of people. The region is also home to a rich biodiversity, with iconic species such as the snow leopard and red panda finding refuge in the valleys and dense forests at its feet.

Kangchenjunga is not only a symbol of natural power, it also embodies the harmony between spirituality and nature. Its imposing stature and mysticism continue to inspire locals, adventurers and mountain lovers the world over, while remaining an unspoilt sanctuary, deeply respected by those who live at its feet.

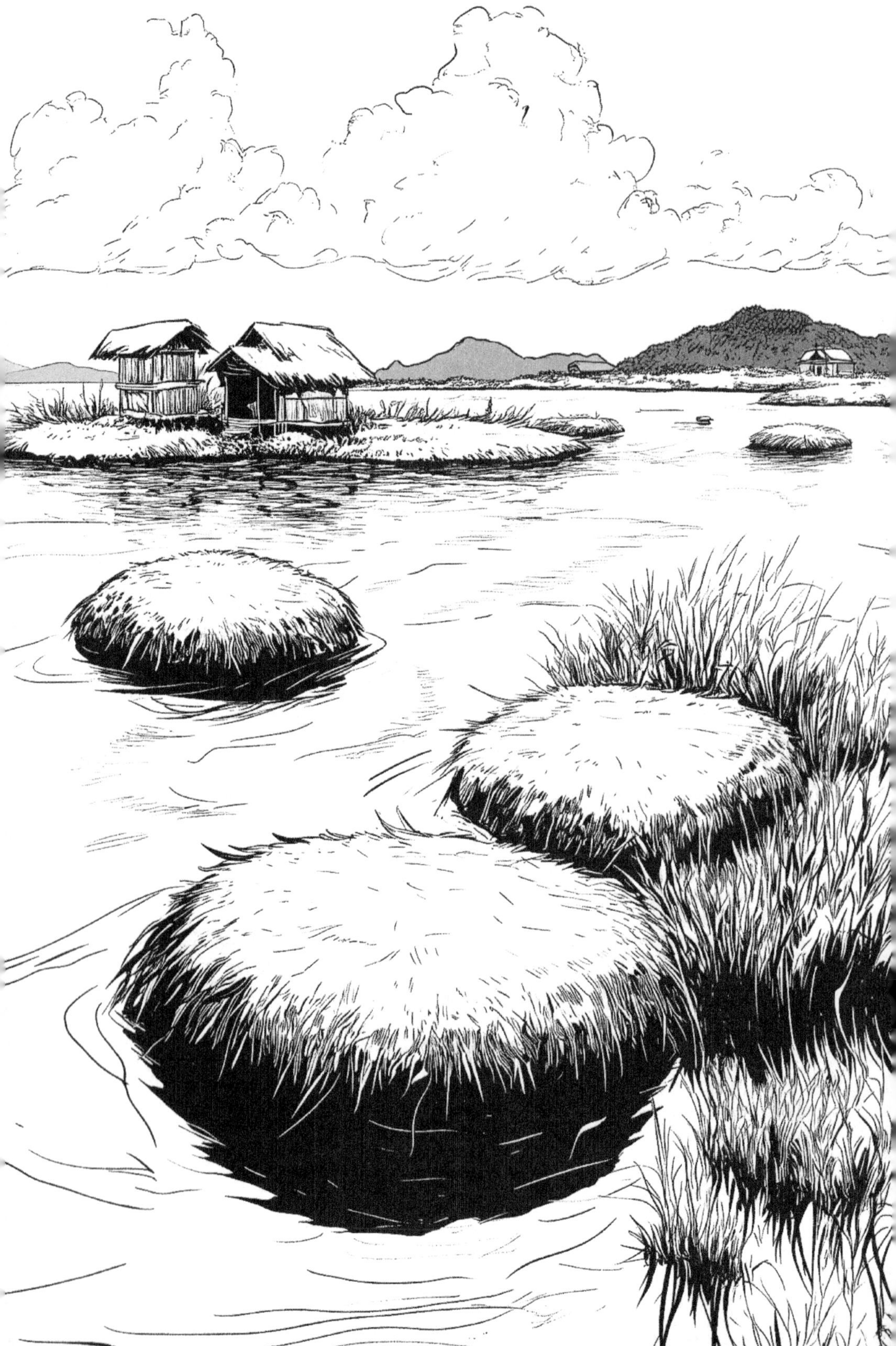

Fact 90 - Lake Loktak is the world's only floating lake

Lake Loktak, located in the Indian state of Manipur, is the only floating lake of its kind in the world. This fascinating phenomenon is made possible by phumdis, floating islands of decomposing organic matter. These phumdis, which vary in size and density, move freely across the surface of the lake, creating a constantly changing landscape. This natural phenomenon has made the lake world-famous, attracting researchers and the curious alike.

Loktak is also vital to the local population. The phumdis are not just natural formations; they provide support for floating dwellings and economic activities such as fishing. The lake's inhabitants use these floating islets to build platforms where they grow crops and raise fish. In this way, Lake Loktak is not only a natural treasure, but also a precious resource for the communities that live around it.

One of the lake's most impressive features is Keibul Lamjao National Park, located on one of the largest phumdis. This park is home to a rare and endangered species, the Manipur deer, or sangai, known for its elegant gait. The park is the only one in the world to float, and is an essential refuge for local wildlife. This exceptional biodiversity further enhances the ecological value of Lake Loktak.

In addition to its natural beauty, Lake Loktak plays a crucial role in the ecological balance of the region. It regulates flooding, provides water for irrigation and domestic consumption, and contributes to the production of hydroelectricity. The lake's unique ecosystems are essential to the preservation of the environment, and its conservation is a priority for local and international authorities.

Lake Loktak, with its floating islets and remarkable biodiversity, remains an exceptional natural jewel in India and the world. Its beauty, ecological importance and cultural value make it a unique place, both for those who live off its resources and for those who come to marvel at its wonders.

Fact 91 - The king cobra detects movement with its tongue

The king cobra, one of the world's most fearsome snakes, has a unique ability to track its prey: it uses its forked tongue to detect movement in its environment. This sensory technique enables it to pick up chemical particles in the air, which it analyzes thanks to a specific organ located on the palate, called the Jacobson's organ. This enables the king cobra to identify sources of danger or food even in total darkness or complex environments.

Unlike many other snakes, the king cobra stands out for its impressive size. It can reach up to 5.5 meters, making it the longest venomous snake in the world. However, despite its size and powerful venom, this snake prefers to avoid conflict with humans. Its hunting methods rely heavily on the finesse of its senses, and its tongue plays a vital role in its orientation.

The king cobra's ability to detect movement via its tongue makes it extremely efficient in its natural habitat. It lives mainly in the dense rainforests and mangroves of India, where thick vegetation often makes vision ineffective. Thanks to this mechanism, the cobra can identify the passage of rodents, lizards and other prey, even when they are a good distance away.

The use of its tongue to detect movement is not limited to hunting. It is also used to spot potential predators, and above all to find a mate during the mating season. This sensory ability gives the king cobra an evolutionary advantage in the wild, enabling it to adapt to its changing environment and survive in difficult conditions.

Despite its fearsome reputation, the king cobra occupies a respected place in Indian culture, often associated with symbols of power and protection. This impressive predator continues to fascinate researchers and naturalists with its intelligence and sensory abilities, testifying to India's rich biodiversity.

Fact 92 - The Sarasvati, India's mythical vanishing river

The Sarasvati is one of India's most mysterious rivers, both in mythology and history. Mentioned in ancient Vedic texts, this river is described as majestic and essential to the spiritual and material life of the civilizations that surrounded it. It is considered a sacred river, like the Ganges, but with the difference that the Sarasvati disappeared several millennia ago, leaving a gaping hole in ancient accounts.

According to the Vedas, the Sarasvati once flowed with impressive force, linking the Himalayan mountains to the ocean. It flowed through fertile regions and was revered by Aryan peoples as the mother of wisdom and knowledge. Yet, despite its cultural and spiritual importance, the river seems to have disappeared as a result of major climatic changes and tectonic movements that have altered its course, leading to its drying up.

Modern archaeological and geological research has attempted to locate the course of the Sarasvati. Using satellite imaging technology, some experts believe they have identified ancient dry riverbeds in north-west India and Pakistan, which may correspond to the ancient course of the Sarasvati. These discoveries support the idea that the river really did exist, but that it gradually disappeared as its tributaries were diverted into the Ganges and Indus rivers.

The disappearance of the Sarasvati had a major impact on the civilizations that depended on its waters. Archaeological sites, such as those of the Indus Valley civilization, suggest that the drying up of this river contributed to the collapse of some of the great cities of the time. The Sarasvati is therefore not only a mythological symbol, but also a key element in understanding environmental and human evolution in ancient India.

Today, Sarasvati lives on in the collective memory and religious narratives of India. It is often evoked in prayers, and its symbolism remains powerful, embodying purity, knowledge and fertility. Although its bed is now dry, its spiritual and cultural influence endures, reminding us of the importance of rivers in Indian history and culture.

Fact 93 - Konark's Sun temple, dedicated to the sun god

The Sun Temple of Konark, located in the state of Odisha, is one of the most impressive architectural masterpieces of ancient India. Built in the 13th century by King Narasimhadeva I of the Eastern Ganga dynasty, this temple is dedicated to the sun god, Surya. It is often compared to a gigantic solar chariot, symbolizing the god's vehicle, drawn by seven horses representing the days of the week.

The architecture of the Konark temple is breathtaking. Its chariot-like shape rests on twelve pairs of beautifully sculpted wheels, each representing the months of the year and the hours of the day. These wheels are not only decorative, they were also used as sundials. This illustrates the skill of ancient Indian architects, who integrated both aesthetic and scientific concepts into their constructions.

The temple is also remarkable for its detailed carvings, which cover almost every surface of the building. These sculptures tell stories of daily life, deities and myths linked to the Sun. In addition to religious scenes, there are artistic and symbolic representations, offering a glimpse into the culture of the time. The brilliance and precision of the sculptures make the Konark Sun Temple a jewel of medieval Indian art.

Sadly, much of the temple is in ruins today. Natural disasters, such as earthquakes, and erosion are thought to have contributed to its deterioration over time. Nevertheless, a significant part of the temple is still standing, and it continues to attract visitors from all over the world for its architectural beauty and spiritual significance.

A UNESCO World Heritage Site, Konark's Sun Temple is not only a symbol of devotion to the sun god, but also a testament to the incredible ingenuity and creativity of ancient Indian craftsmen. This monument, which combines art, religion and astronomy, remains a source of wonder for all who visit it.

Fact 94 - Andaman tribes are among the most isolated in the world

The Andaman Islands in the Indian Ocean are home to some of the world's most isolated and ancient tribes. Among them, the Sentinelese and the Onge stand out for their extreme isolation. These indigenous groups have lived for millennia with almost no contact with the outside world, preserving their ancestral lifestyles and customs. Their way of life, still largely based on hunting and gathering, remains a fascinating window on human societies that have remained intact in the face of modernity.

The Sentinels, who live on the island of North Sentinel, are particularly notorious for their categorical refusal of all outside contact. They fiercely defend their territory and communicate with the outside world only through demonstrations of force. Little is known about their culture, language or practices, as all attempts to approach them have been rebuffed. This fierce protection of their territory makes them one of the last uncontacted peoples on Earth, and they continue to live without outside influence.

The Indian government has taken strict measures to protect these isolated tribes, forbidding any attempt at contact with the Sentinels, due to the risk of transmitting diseases to which they have no immunity. These tribes, like the Onge, are also protected by law to preserve their unique culture and traditional way of life. These protection policies aim to let them live in harmony with their natural environment, far from the disturbances of the modern world.

The culture of the Andaman tribes is marked by an in-depth knowledge of their environment. They depend entirely on nature for their survival, whether for food, shelter or the tools they use. This intimate relationship with nature enables them to survive in difficult conditions to which many could not adapt.

The tribes of the Andaman Islands are a living testimony to human and cultural diversity. Their existence reminds us that there are still pockets of people living outside modern civilization, leading an existence that their ancestors would have recognized. These groups are often seen as custodians of an ancient way of life in balance with nature, and their protection is essential to the preservation of the world's cultural and human diversity.

Fact 95 - Mehrangarh fort has remained impregnable for centuries

Mehrangarh Fort, located in Jodhpur, Rajasthan, is one of India's most imposing fortresses. Perched on a hill 122 meters above the city, this imposing bastion is famous for its impregnability, remaining inviolate since its construction in the 15th century by Rao Jodha, the founder of Jodhpur. The fort's massive 36-metre-high walls have withstood the most violent assaults, ensuring the city's security through the ages.

The architecture of Mehrangarh Fort, with its seven gates, is a living testimony to the ingenuity of the craftsmen and engineers of yesteryear. Each gate was built to repel elephant and cannon attacks, and some, like the "Jayapol" (victory gate), celebrate military victories against invading armies. Legend has it that even the most powerful neighboring kingdoms failed to breach these impressive defenses.

The ramparts offer spectacular views of the blue city of Jodhpur and hint at the splendor of this ancient capital. Inside the fort, sumptuous palaces such as the Phool Mahal (Palace of Flowers) and the Sheesh Mahal (Palace of Mirrors) illustrate the wealth and grandeur of the rulers of Marwar. Mehrangarh's fine carvings and architectural details make it a jewel of Rajput architecture.

The fort also houses museums displaying weapons, royal costumes and precious objects linked to the region's history. Mehrangarh's history is not just military, it's also cultural, with tales of kings who were patrons of the arts and protectors of tradition. The fort remains a symbol of the power of the Rathores, the dynasty that ruled Jodhpur.

Today, Mehrangarh is a major tourist attraction, but it still retains an aura of mystery and invincibility. Visitors feel the strength and history that permeate every stone, and understand why, after centuries, this fortress remains impregnable, defying the passage of time.

Fact 96 - India has the longest national highway, NH44

National Highway 44 (NH44) is India's longest national highway, linking the northern and southern ends of the country. This vital artery stretches for some 3,745 kilometers, from Srinagar in Jammu and Kashmir to Kanyakumari in the far south of Tamil Nadu. Crossing a multitude of states and varied landscapes, the NH44 connects key cities such as Delhi, Hyderabad and Bangalore, while playing a crucial role in the transport of goods and passengers.

The NH44 route crosses a variety of terrains, from the Himalayan mountains in the north to the central plains and tropical regions of the south. Travelers on this route can observe a diversity of climates and cultures as they pass through modern urban areas and traditional villages. This journey is a perfect illustration of India's geographical and cultural richness.

In terms of infrastructure, the NH44 has undergone major modernization, including track widening and the construction of bypasses to ease traffic flow, particularly in densely populated urban areas. Bridge and tunnel projects, such as the Chenani-Nashri tunnel in Jammu and Kashmir, have been carried out to improve travel conditions in mountainous regions.

This road also plays a strategic role in the Indian economy. It connects major economic and industrial centers, facilitating the rapid transport of goods across the country. The NH44's role is therefore vital for trade and logistics, as well as for travelers seeking to discover the different regions of India.

The NH44 is not just a road, but a true link between the different cultures, histories and landscapes that make up India. For intrepid travelers, it offers a unique adventure through spectacular scenery, illustrating the breadth of India's diversity with every kilometer traveled.

Fact 97 - The Kumbh Mela gathers 100 million people

The Kumbh Mela is the world's largest religious gathering, attracting almost 100 million pilgrims at its peak. This sacred Hindu event takes place every 12 years in four Indian cities: Allahabad (now Prayagraj), Haridwar, Nashik and Ujjain. It marks a period of spiritual purification, when devotees bathe in the sacred waters of the Ganges, Yamuna and mythical Sarasvati rivers.

The origins of the Kumbh Mela go back to ancient legends linked to the quest for immortality. According to Hindu mythology, during the battle between the gods and demons for the nectar of immortality, some of this precious liquid fell to four places on earth, giving rise to these sacred sites. This age-old tradition attracts millions of people in search of blessings and spiritual fulfillment.

The logistics involved in organizing the Kumbh Mela are impressive. Temporary infrastructures are set up to accommodate the pilgrims, including hospitals, camps and reinforced transport networks. Coordination between local and national authorities is essential to ensure the safety and management of such a huge crowd, which can reach up to 30 million people in a single day.

For sadhus, Hindu ascetics often dressed in ashes and flower garlands, the Kumbh Mela is a key moment in their spiritual life. Their rituals, including spectacular processions and sacred baths, capture the attention of participants. These moments of collective devotion have a unique religious intensity, and leave a deep impression on all who attend.

Beyond its spiritual significance, this massive gathering is also a symbol of the diversity and religious fervor that characterize India. The Kumbh Mela embodies unity in diversity, with pilgrims coming from all parts of the country, transcending social, linguistic and cultural differences, to celebrate a common belief in purification and devotion.

Fact 98 - Holi, the world-famous festival of colors

Holi, one of India's most emblematic festivals, is celebrated every year with the arrival of spring. Known as the "festival of colors", it is marked by an explosion of bright pigments hurled into the streets by joyful crowds. The festival is deeply symbolic: it celebrates the victory of good over evil, notably through the story of Prahlad and Holika, central figures in Hindu mythology. On the eve of Holi, a large pyre called "Holika Dahan" is lit to symbolize this victory.

Holi festivities are a veritable explosion of color and conviviality. In India, everyone participates, regardless of age, caste or social status. On the day itself, the streets are transformed into scenes of collective joy as people throw colored powders, called gulal, at each other while spraying each other with water. Traditional songs and dances punctuate these moments, while festival-goers enjoy sweets such as gujiyas and drinks made from spiced milk.

The origins of Holi lie in legends linked to the god Krishna, whose mischievous games with Radha and the gopis, the young shepherdesses, inspired the tradition of throwing colors. Krishna, being dark-skinned, had a complex about Radha's fair skin, and his mother suggested he color Radha's face to even out their skin tones. This joyful interaction gave rise to one of the festival's best-known practices.

Beyond India, Holi has taken on a global dimension. Today, festivals inspired by this tradition are held in many countries, attracting millions of participants fascinated by the symbolism of color and unity. The festival has become a symbol of international celebration of diversity, joy and renewal, embodying the spirit of fraternity across cultural boundaries.

Holi is much more than just a festival of colors. It's a time of reconciliation, when quarrels are forgotten, and friends and families come together to express their love and gratitude. The festival offers a unique opportunity to renew ties and put past tensions behind us, making it an essential celebration of living together in India and around the world.

Fact 99 - The Thar Desert is home to desert foxes

The Thar Desert, located mainly in the Indian state of Rajasthan, is one of the world's most diverse desert ecosystems. Despite its arid appearance, it is home to a unique fauna, including the desert fox, or Bengal fox, a species perfectly adapted to the extreme conditions of this region. These foxes are renowned for their small size, large ears and ability to survive on little water, deriving their hydration mainly from their food.

In addition to their adaptation to the heat, desert foxes are skilful nocturnal hunters. They feed on small mammals, reptiles and insects, which are abundant despite the arid conditions. At night, when temperatures drop, these foxes emerge from their burrows in search of food, avoiding the intense heat of the day. Their keen hearing and agile legs enable them to locate their prey with great precision, even in the dark.

Their light coat plays an important role in their survival, helping them to camouflage themselves in the sand dunes of the Thar. This coat color not only enables them to escape predators, but also to regulate body temperature by reflecting some of the sun's heat. Their large ears not only improve their hearing, but also help dissipate heat.

The presence of these foxes in the Thar Desert testifies to the resilience of the local fauna in the face of harsh environmental conditions. Although humans have colonized much of the Thar, these animals have managed to preserve their territory in the more remote, protected areas of the desert, notably in the Desert National Park, where biodiversity is conserved. Conservation efforts are essential to protect these species from habitat loss and increasing threats.

The desert fox symbolizes the hidden beauty of this arid environment, where life persists despite the challenges. The Thar Desert, with its unique diversity and resilient inhabitants, offers a powerful lesson in adaptation and survival, even in the most inhospitable places.

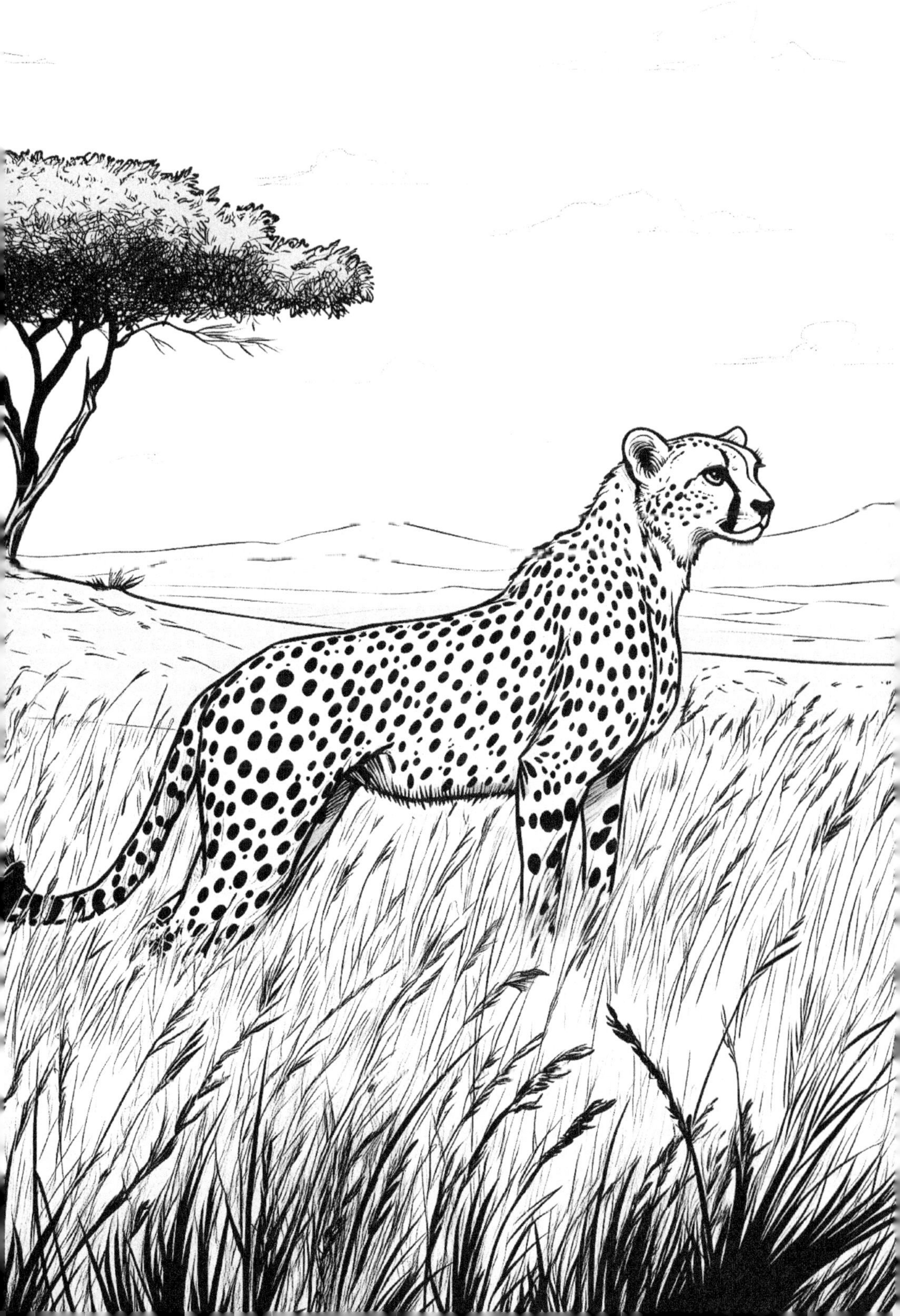

Fact 100 - The cheetah reintroduced in India after 70 years

The cheetah, once present in India, disappeared from the country in 1952, a victim of excessive hunting and the loss of its natural habitat. However, after an absence of 70 years, India reintroduced this emblematic species to its territory in 2022, marking a historic moment for biodiversity conservation. The cheetah, recognized as the fastest land animal, occupies an important place in the ecosystem as a predator at the top of the food chain.

This reintroduction project required years of preparation and international collaboration. Cheetahs from Namibia were released in Kuno National Park, a site carefully selected for its biodiversity and ability to support the species. This park, located in the state of Madhya Pradesh, offers an ideal habitat with vast open plains, conducive to rapid cheetah hunting.

The reintroduction of the cheetah in India is part of a wider drive to restore original ecosystems and wildlife diversity. The cheetah plays an essential role in regulating prey populations, thus promoting ecological balance. The project is also symbolic, underlining India's efforts to reverse the trend of extinction and protect endangered species.

The cheetah has always had a special place in Indian history and culture. The Mughal emperors, fascinated by this animal, even used it for hunting. Its return to India, after decades, is a reminder of the ancient link between this species and the subcontinent, while giving renewed hope to the preservation of global biodiversity.

This reintroduction project is a clear example of India's ongoing wildlife conservation efforts, a commitment to protecting and recovering extinct species while ensuring their coexistence with ecosystems and human communities.

Conclusion

Here you are, at the end of this journey through 100 Amazing Facts about India. I hope these discoveries have helped you appreciate the richness and diversity of this fascinating country. Whether you've browsed these pages out of curiosity or to deepen your knowledge, India has surely revealed some of its wonders through its history, culture and extraordinary nature.

Beyond the monuments and landscapes you've discovered, the depths of the Indian soul are revealed. India is the incredible cohabitation of the old and the new, where age-old customs find their place alongside technological advances. It's a nation that defies expectations and shows that past and future can come together harmoniously.

India is not just a place to explore; it's an experience to live. Behind every Fact are stories of people, traditions and beliefs that have endured through the ages and continue to shape everyday life. From the dazzling celebrations of Holi to silent monuments like the Taj Mahal, every aspect of India tells a unique story.

By the end of this adventure, you'll have realized that India is much more than just a country on the map. It's an entire universe of cultures, languages, philosophies and landscapes that never ceases to amaze those who discover it. Every region, every city, every community has something to offer and something to tell, turning every visit into a new revelation.

As you close this book, keep in mind that India is an infinite land of discovery. Whether through its stories, its flavors, or its panoramas, this country continues to inspire and fascinate. Perhaps one day you'll have the chance to set foot here and see for yourself the splendor of this incredible nation.

Marc Dresqui

Quiz

1) What is the main soil composition of the Deccan Plateau?

- a) Granite
- b) Sand
- c) Basalt
- d) Clay

2) Why does the Taj Mahal change color throughout the day?

- a) Because of the reflections from the minarets
- b) Because of air pollution
- c) Thanks to the special quality of the white marble used, which reflects light in a unique way
- d) Due to the position of the gardens

3) What is the main reason why ghee is preferred for high-temperature cooking?

- a) It contains fewer calories than other oils
- b) It has a distinctly sweet taste
- c) It does not decompose easily and retains its benefits
- d) More economical than other fats

4) What do geologists and historians believe is the main reason for the disappearance of the Sarasvati River?

- a) It has been absorbed by a larger river
- b) It was blocked by dams built in ancient times.
- c) Climate change and tectonic movements have dried it out
- d) It was redirected to the Pacific Ocean

5) Which mythological event is mainly commemorated during the Holi festival?

- a) The birth of the god Krishna
- b) The wedding of Rama and Sita
- c) Prahlad's miraculous escape from the fire lit by his Aunt Holika
- d) The creation of the first temple dedicated to Vishnu

6) Which emblematic animal species attracts international attention at Kaziranga National Park?

- a) The Asian elephant
- b) The Bengal tiger
- c) The one-horned rhinoceros
- d) The wild buffalo

7) What is the name of India's first mission to Mars, launched in 2013?
- a) Chandrayaan
- b) Mars Voyager
- c) Mangalyaan
- d) AstroSat

8) What is the main role played by Sundarbans mangroves in the ecosystem?
- a) They increase water salinity.
- b) They protect mountains from erosion.
- c) They naturally filter water, removing impurities.
- d) They create stronger tides in the region.

9) Which country produces the largest quantity of curry and the spices needed to make it?
- a) China
- b) Thailand
- c) India
- d) Japan

10) Where is the world's largest Hindu temple, Akshardham, located?
- a) Mumbai
- b) Bangalore
- c) Varanasi
- d) Delhi

11) What does the sacred "rakhi" thread tied around the wrist during the Raksha Bandhan festival symbolize?
- a) A prayer for prosperity
- b) A promise of eternal friendship
- c) A prayer for your brother's protection
- d) A promise of loyalty

12) How high is the Qûtb Minâr, India's tallest brick minaret?
- a) 45 meters
- b) 60 meters
- c) 73 metres
- d) 85 metres

13) What is the traditional Indian samosa joke?
- a) Cheese and tomatoes
- b) Spicy potatoes and peas
- c) Rice and lentils
- d) Fish and vegetables

14) Which tribe in the Andaman Islands is known for avoiding all outside contact and firmly defending its territory?

   a) Les Onges
   b) The Nicobars
   c) The Jarawas
   d) The Sentinels

15) Which famous grammarian codified the grammar of classical Sanskrit?

   a) Vyasa
   b) Valmiki
   c) Panini
   d) Kalidasa

16) What mountain range borders Ladakh in northern India?

   a) The Western Ghats
   b) The Aravalli Mountains
   c) Himalayas and Karakoram
   d) The Nilgiri Mountains

17) What is Aryabhata's major contribution to mathematics?

   a) Discovering the decimal system
   b) The invention of trigonometry
   c) The discovery of zero
   d) Creating quadratic equations

18) What makes Lake Loktak unique in the world?

   a) It is located at the highest altitude in the world
   b) India's largest salt lake
   c) The world's only floating lake
   d) It is surrounded by mountains

19) Why has Mehrangarh Fort been famous ever since it was built?

   a) It's located on the edge of the ocean
   b) It was transformed into a royal palace
   c) It has remained impregnable for centuries
   d) It is made entirely of gold

20) Where did the cheetahs reintroduced to India after a 70-year absence come from?

   a) From South Africa
   b) From Ethiopia
   c) From Namibia
   d) From Tanzania

Answers

1) What is the main soil composition of the Deccan Plateau?

Correct answer: c) Basalt

2) Why does the Taj Mahal change color throughout the day?

Correct answer: c) Thanks to the special quality of the white marble used, which reflects light in a unique way.

3) What is the main reason why ghee is preferred for high-temperature cooking?

Correct answer: c) It does not decompose easily and retains its benefits.

4) What do geologists and historians believe is the main reason for the disappearance of the Sarasvati River?

Correct answer: c) Climate change and tectonic movements have dried it out.

5) Which mythological event is mainly commemorated during the Holi festival?

Correct answer: c) Prahlad's miraculous escape from the fire lit by his aunt Holika

6) Which emblematic animal species attracts international attention at Kaziranga National Park?

Correct answer: c) One-horned rhinoceros

7) What is the name of India's first mission to Mars, launched in 2013?

Correct answer: c) Mangalyaan

8) What is the main role played by Sundarbans mangroves in the ecosystem?

Correct answer: c) They naturally filter water, removing impurities.

9) Which country produces the largest quantity of curry and the spices needed to make it?

Correct answer: c) India

10) Where is the world's largest Hindu temple, Akshardham, located?

Correct answer: d) Delhi

11) What does the sacred "rakhi" thread tied around the wrist during the Raksha Bandhan festival symbolize?

Correct answer: c) A prayer for the brother's protection

12) How high is the Qûtb Minâr, India's tallest brick minaret?

Correct answer: c) 73 metres

13) What is the traditional Indian samosa joke?

Correct answer: b) Spiced potatoes and peas

14) Which tribe in the Andaman Islands is known for avoiding all outside contact and firmly defending its territory?

Correct answer: d) Sentinels

15) Which famous grammarian codified the grammar of classical Sanskrit?

Correct answer: c) Panini

16) What mountain range borders Ladakh in northern India?

Correct answer: c) Himalayas and Karakoram

17) What is Aryabhata's major contribution to mathematics?

Correct answer: c) The discovery of zero

18) What makes Lake Loktak unique in the world?

Correct answer: c) It's the world's only floating lake.

19) Why has Mehrangarh Fort been famous ever since it was built?

Correct answer: c) It has remained impregnable for centuries.

20) Where did the cheetahs reintroduced to India after a 70-year absence come from?

Correct answer: c) From Namibia

Printed in Great Britain
by Amazon